THE BOY WHO
NEVER CRIED WOLF

By grace he survived ten years with a child predator.
By providence he now hunts them

Detective James B. Wischer, Jr.

WESTBOW
PRESS
A DIVISION OF THOMAS NELSON

WestBow Press books may be ordered through booksellers or by contacting:

WestBow Press
A Division of Thomas Nelson
1663 Liberty Drive
Bloomington, IN 47403
www.westbowpress.com
1-(866) 928-1240

Because of the dynamic nature of the Internet, any web addresses or links contained in this book may have changed since publication and may no longer be valid. The views expressed in this work are solely those of the author and do not necessarily reflect the views of the publisher, and the publisher hereby disclaims any responsibility for them.

Any people depicted in stock imagery provided by Thinkstock are models, and such images are being used for illustrative purposes only.

Certain stock imagery © Thinkstock.

ISBN: 978-1-4497-5259-0 (sc)
ISBN: 978-1-4497-5260-6 (hc)
ISBN: 978-1-4497-5258-3 (e)

Library of Congress Control Number: 2012908916

Printed in the United States of America

WestBow Press rev. date: 10/16/2012

Genesis 50:20
"You intended to harm me, but God intended it for good to accomplish what is <u>now</u> being done, the saving of many lives."

CONTENTS

FORWARD

IN 1968 I WAS A 21 years old police officer in the City of Toronto, Canada. In the few years I served on the 'job' I never once heard of a child predator. In fact, I could not have even imagined anyone doing to a child what now seems so common. When I read the statistics that Jim mentions in this book I realized just how big a problem sexual molestation really is. Jim's book is gripping from the opening pages. As you read this incredibly brave story you will be horrified at what happened to a young innocent child, but you will also laugh as Jim describes some of the funny things that happened in his life journey. I can promise you who read this book that your life will be impacted in several ways. If you have experienced a similar life event you will be filled with hope that your life can truly be happy again. If you are bitter and angry at God you will read instead how God intervenes in the midst of one of life's true injustices. You will read of the incredible power of forgiveness to free your life from the nightmare of the past. I recently traveled with Jim to Siberia to minister with him in some churches. I will never forget the profound impact of Jim's preaching about forgiveness. We in the congregations sat spellbound listening to a man who had experienced the deliverance that only comes from an authentic relationship with Jesus. As a Christ follower I believe it is my responsibility to reach out to others in need in my community. Jim has now alerted me to a need I did not realize was so crucial and common. It is my hope and prayer that this book will be widely read by Pastors and Law Enforcement and many others who may care deeply about the children who are the future of our culture. You will laugh and cry and be surprised at the wonderful intervention of our loving Father in Jim's life and you will be confident in knowing He will come to your rescue as well. I could not recommend this book too highly. It will certainly begin as a best seller in our congregation; Calvary Chapel of Sarasota. It is my hope; "The Boy Who Never Cried Wolf" will have a great impact on the lives of many all over our great land.

Pastor Carl Dixon, Calvary Chapel of Sarasota

INTRODUCTION

AN AWFUL PRESENCE FILLED THE room and before I could draw another breath, it had seized me. With devilish claws it dragged me down to a place where all peace seemed to abandon me. I was trapped and struggled to breath. Paralyzed by the heaviness of this thing, I literally felt my life being suffocated out of me. In my panic I strained to eek out a whisper, "Where am I"? My mind labored to make some sense of the scene that I had just been hurled into, but my eyes proved too weak to focus. It was so dark. I was cold and I don't mind telling you I was more than a little afraid. Then in the haze, just beyond my vision, he began to take form. With one vile word I instantly knew where I was. I had, in fact, been in this dank colorless place numerous times and had been subject to his tyranny more times than I could remember. His words were bitter and well rehearsed. "Jimmy, if you ever tell anyone about this I will kill your mommy and you will never see her again! Do you understand me? You will never see her again!" Sporting that familiar depraved glare, he towered over me and spewed his venom. As I shrank back in terror, I could not help feeling as small and helpless as a mouse. Oh my God, I thought to myself, it's happening again! With his toxic threats now bouncing off the inner walls of my skull like so many thorns, my heart spiked to near critical. I tried to resist, but could summons no strength in which to save myself. There was no use; I couldn't even lift my head from the ground. With that one final desperate realization, I began to gently sink into what appeared to be another inevitable and horrible attack. As this spectacle reached its horrific crescendo, I braced myself for the coming onslaught and allowed my fearful heart to silently plea "Dear Jesus, come and help me". Oh what power must reside in that name. What terror the darkness must feel from His fiery gaze, for with that one little whimpering squeak for help it all just suddenly stopped. Just like that the pressure relented and the darkness retreated. A deep cool cleansing breath rushed into my empty lungs and freed them from their burning prison. Peace and joy were returning. The tears and sweat, which were now soaking my face and pillow, began to graciously shake me free from my slumber and from the horrible ghosts of my past. I sat straight up in my bed and labored to catch my breath. As the pounding rhythm in my chest began to calm, I just stared at myself in the mirror. It seemed pitiful that I should still be wrestling with that same nightmare at my age, but there it was. My eyes cleared and I caught a glimpse of the hair clinging to my head. I looked like a man who had just crawled out of a river of sweat. As I took stock of my 200 pound frame, the fear began to vaporize as quickly as it had arrived. I simply brushed it off and grinned at the devil. But in reality, he had just stolen another valuable night of sleep and I was left to wonder why those awful feelings of vulnerability and fear, which seemed so real in my unconscious state, were still visiting me. What ever the reason, I didn't know if I could take it much longer. I mean, God Almighty! Was this thing going to chase me forever?

It was otherwise a typically blissful mid-Spring morning in 2007 at my home in Southwest Florida. The sun was already well on its cycle heavenward and by all accounts it should have been another beautiful day in paradise. The comedic sound of our neighbor's cat being teased by a pair of local mocking birds seemed to foster a sense of envy that I too wasn't out there embracing the day. The rustle of warm tropical wind through the palms trees brought only further provocation and from that moment on the day should have been mine to seize. However, with this fire storm raging inside of me as it was and with the sweat still fresh on my face, this particular morning would not be so typical. For this would be the morning in which I found myself awaking to the overwhelming birth pains of this project. Its water had now broken and the contractions were mere moments apart. No matter how fervently I wished to procrastinate further, I found myself quite unable to forbear any longer the persistent unction to put pen to paper and chronicle these sad and felonious events. Despite their disturbing nature and despite having spanned back a full thirty five years, these long hidden crimes were about to be forced into the light. Particularly noteworthy--and quite possibly the principle reason for no longer holding the knowledge of these crimes in secret--was the testimony of my survival and of their absolute failure in preventing me from truly becoming one of the happiest men alive.

The extraordinary seasons of my life have hastened along largely unnoticed and have silently documented the manifest tragedy of my journey along the way. Looking back at the absolute haste of their comings and goings, I fear that I have caught only mere glimpses of their memorable contents as they passed me by. The lost time and bad memories not withstanding, these seasons have dutifully and faithfully ushered me to the present, now stronger and wiser than in my youth and even now hold their peace as I fast approach middle age. I am forty one years old and it is at this very moment that I find myself standing in the light of a new and fantastic liberation; one which refuses to be denied the light of day any longer. Picture the sweetest release you've ever known and you will have only come close to knowing the ecstasy that is now mine. I have likened the whole experience to that of some poor exhausted degenerate, who after a life time of being tossed about on some stormy ocean, had at long last found himself emerging from the stomach of that sickening fog and into the warm daylight. With nothing left but calm seas and a calm mind, I found myself staring straight into those brilliant beams of radiant warmth inviting them to press hard against my tired face. Finally, hope stirred; glorious hope, a hope of at last leaving the darkness far behind. This condemning mist which had shackled me for most of my life was none other than the dread fog *shame* and *denial*. This beast had literally veiled and crippled my mind for decades and had quite successfully prevented me from living my life in a manner which most take for granted. It had also denied me the freedom of helping others who were currently suffering the same calamity that I had suffered. But, to my surprise, the prevailing winds of time and grace began to blow this fog away. Providence is shining itself brightly upon me and I am seeing things more clearly now than ever before. It was truly an instantaneous epiphany. On April the first, 2007, it simply occurred to me that I was in fact free to do what needed to have been done decades earlier. For thirty five years I had quite literally never uttered a single word of what had happened to my siblings and me as children, other than very generically stating that we had been "horribly abused". But to lay out the naked truth was unthinkable. I mean, my God, who could bear to hear such things and remain unchanged in the way they felt about me? Well, for better or for worse, the time has come for this story and all of its ugliness to be dragged from its dank hiding place and stripped of its power.

Many of the horrifying events that are revealed within the pages of the following chapters are recorded just as they happened to me and may not be suitable for younger readers. Please know that I never intended to sound grotesque simply for the sake of sounding that way. But, unfortunately, the heinous acts which were committed against me and my siblings were by their very nature grotesque and will undoubtedly be viewed as such. I will also let you know here that although this story is absolutely true in its entirety, I have, for obvious reasons of protecting the innocent, taken the liberty of changing most of the names of the people involved.

I am currently a law enforcement officer in the community where I reside with my wife and son. My time spent as a deputy sheriff and even now as a detective with our agency's division on crimes against children has afforded me a rich education in regards to the subject of child sex offenders and their victims. I have literally interviewed, arrested and participated in the prosecution of more men and women in regards to these crimes than you can believe and each week new cases keep arriving. As I now understand it, the crimes which were perpetrated in my family actually occur far more frequently than even I could have imagined and too often go unreported. I don't know how we as a people have allowed this stealthy plague to advance right under our noses as arrogantly as it has; but one thing is certain, every day that passes, young lives are being wrecked almost beyond repair and there seems to be no end in sight.

Now in stark contrast to this, I believe that I live in one of the finest societies in the world. I mean, really, have there ever been a people as compassionate toward human suffering as the people in this great land? I think not. But it should also be pointed out that this tremendous strength of ours seems to have married itself to a much softer side, as we are also a society which does not like to set its gaze on horrible things. If you don't know what I mean by that, just go to the next gory movie that comes along and try not to turn your head during the awful, bloody, scary parts. Having been raised in this society, I completely sympathize with this common reflex and have carried those same reluctant tendencies throughout my life as well. Unfortunately for me, in my current occupation I have to see horrible things. I cringe as I say it, but I usually see more in one week than most people may see in a lifetime and still my senses have never dulled to the pain of seeing them. I constantly have to fight that natural urge to turn away from those agonizing scenes which we keep discretely hidden from the public behind our yellow police tape. Perhaps it is that panging urge of our conscience which guides us and compels us to avert our eyes, so that our hearts may be spared the pain. But it is to your very conscience that I must now appeal and ask that you not turn away from what I am putting before you. Please let me assure you that although these revelations may read like a horror film, this is not fiction. It is in fact one of the most damnable sins to ever visit itself upon a society and it simply must be seen for what it really is. I know that once these horrible crimes against children have been completely exposed, we will better know how to deal with them. It's just that exposing them has always been the difficult part of the equation. My sincere hope is that when the light shines on this thing, we will all see it and feel the urge to address it. That with one mighty voice we would cry out on behalf of those who cannot cry out for themselves; and believe me, they are desperately awaiting such an outcry.

Not too many years ago, if my memory serves me correctly, I heard a story that was really worth the telling. Although I can no longer be certain of its origin, I believe I saw it on the evening news. Anyway, it was a most heroic story which came out of the carnage in Iraq. An Iraqi gentleman was telling of his son whom he had recently lost just prior to the invasion of coalition forces. His son, who was in his early twenties, had been arrested by Saddam's secret police and accused of who knows what. It was not long before the father was contacted and told that his son was dead. The cold, heartless voice at the other end of the line instructed the broken man to retrieve his son's body if he wanted it. The man located his son's lifeless corpse exactly where the voice had instructed. The young man's naked body was bruised, cut, broken and bore all of those familiar burn marks of a man who had recently been tortured to death. Everyone in town knew very well that this man's son had been arrested and would probably not survive the ordeal. But none of them could prove these atrocities or would dare cry out against this dangerous government, for fear of the same. This father, who was now burning with anger and against every loving instinct to hide his son's shame, did the unexpected. He carried his son just as he had found him into the town square and laid his naked, tortured body before the eyes of the entire city. Now, in the glaring light of this awful truth, no one could deny what had happened and what was occurring at the hands of these worthless fellows. This man must have been dying on the inside as he did this, but he knew that there would surely be more victims if he held his peace. I know that his neighbors found it simply hideous to gaze at the specter of this murdered son. But they all knew very well what was being revealed and said nothing as they privately rejoiced in his bravery.

By laying out my own tortured past before the eyes of the world, I hope to accomplish something of the same with this little book. Regardless of our political affiliation, I think that we all rejoiced in our own way, at the violent down fall of Saddam's murderous regime. After seeing all of those dead Kurdish civilians and the mass graves on our televisions night after night, how could we not? Or after gazing at those horrifying scenes of the babies lying in the streets after having just been gassed, who of us could restrain our hatred? I know perfectly well that there were probably darker political forces at work also, I'm not naive. But I'll bet that none of us shed a single tear when the hangman sent that lunatic to his grave. In like manner we feel the same when we witness criminals here at home receiving justice for having perpetrated dreadful crimes against innocent victims. We especially feel it when those victims are young children who can do nothing to rescue themselves from such horror. But since we do not like to look at such things and since they are not placed before our eyes as much as the seemingly larger international affairs, I feel it prudent for me to now follow the example of that brave Iraqi father and lend my voice and my story to their cause.

As I type these words hundreds, perhaps even thousands of children are being brutally raped, molested, tortured and threatened all across this country. Some of these little ones will simply lose their lives today. Statistics suggest that as many as one out of every five boys and girls will be sexually abused in some way by the time they turn eighteen. All I can think to say when I hear this is: are you kidding me? It is now known that much of this will occur at the hands of people who are very close to these children and not merely random opportunistic strangers (although that occurs as well). It will often occur at the hands of the very people who are supposed to be caring for and protecting them. People who are close enough to keep these crimes well hidden for long periods of time, while keeping the children so terrified that they may never utter a word in their own defense. These crimes may be occurring next door to you and, if you do not know what you are looking for, may simply go unnoticed. This was the case for me and my siblings for nearly our entire childhoods. Now some will doubtlessly raise a concern that such a proactive stance may unduly injure or offend a neighbor who is guilty of no wrong doing. I know. I get it. And I really do hope that no one turns this information into some mindless, hysteric witch hunt. That would be most counterproductive and not at all what I am wishing to accomplish here. I know that these misguided attention seekers will immerge onto the scene anyway, but I am also certain that their numbers are far too few to simply ignore or abandon the cause. I feel that with a little good information and encouragement most people will be eager to help pull these children from the flames that are burning them alive. Of course no one likes to be the one who rocks the proverbial boat, especially one shrouded in uncertainty. But if by offering an account of the ugly events of my childhood lends assistance to people of good will and helps them understand what to look for, then it will be worth the time and humiliation. Maybe then we can begin to rock the right boats.

There was another national headline story, not long ago, regarding a young boy who had been abducted by a stranger. If I remember correctly, a description of the kidnapper and his vehicle had been given to local police, who quickly released the information to the press. Someone who knew the kidnapper happened to be watching the news and heard the description. They of course contacted the police and asked them to investigate. It turned out that they were right and within no time, the abducted boy was located at the kidnapper's apartment. He was then rescued and returned to his anxious family. The kidnapper was also apprehended shortly there after and was taken to jail. But the story then took a turn for the bizarre. While rescuing the boy from the apartment, the police located a second boy who had been abducted in much the same way, only years earlier. This second boy, who was now fourteen years old, appeared to be living a "normal" life with his abductor. There were stories of him riding his bicycle to school regularly, spending the night with friends and carrying on normal relationships with other children his age. The obvious questions immediately surfaced. Why did this boy, who had now been living with his abductor for years, never take any of these apparent opportunities to tell someone what had happened to him or cry out for help or run to a phone and call his parents. What kept this boy silent for all of those years? That, my friend, is the million dollar question. While most media types seemed happy and sympathetic toward the boy and his family, one could not help but sense the bewilderment which was now showing on some of their faces. What was it that kept this obviously healthy and intelligent boy quiet? What indeed? Now I have never met this boy, but I can tell you for a fact, that I know the answer to that riddle. I know why he stayed quiet. Having endured more than ten years of my own similar hell, I know exactly why he remained silent. After having twenty five more years to consider it all, I feel certain that I am now able to help people find answers to such puzzling questions. Answers that may help rescue someone like him years earlier and also from the inner torment which will certainly follow. The fact is, that if this child had not been found and if he had simply been left in his hellish circumstance and if his abductor had not eventually murdered him, he would have become old enough to free himself in due time. Some time after that he would probably have decided to seek justice for the horrible wrongs committed against him. If during that season he were again left alone, his anger and humiliation may overwhelm him. They would probably turn to rage or self destructive habits which could drag on for decades before he finally found justice and true healing.

Ironically, these young victims are surrounded every day by an army of kind souls, any one of whom could be their hero. Coaches, teachers, neighbors and family, each one passing them by day after day, while their hollow eyes beg for someone to notice their torment and save them. These are the things that I personally wished for while growing up, but never received. I witnessed ten years of the faces of people who knew me and my siblings and while looking at us and suspecting that something was dreadfully wrong, refused to dig any deeper. Now that I am an adult and a father myself, I fully understand their apprehension and certainly do not wish to see anyone hastily attack another with foolish, uninformed accusations. But armed with knowledge and the right tools, we can successfully rescue *children* who are actually being tormented right now. Is this cause not nobler than that of rescuing trees or owls? I agree that trees and whales and owls are all good causes as well. But surely you would agree that the rescue of these defenseless little ones is far more meritorious. I don't want to see the disappearance of these other things, but children are our very future and surely deserve far more of our undivided attention and energy than these other crusades ever will. They deserve no less than a full court press on our part to secure for them the salvation which they could in no way procure for themselves. With this same energy, we can also assist the adults who have lived to escape on their own and who could certainly use our help on their journey to wholeness. These scandalous crimes have remained in the dark for far too long. My sincere prayer is that my story will shine some light that will help rescue the ones who need it. I pray also that it will guide the ones who wish to assist in the fight for their rescue. But most importantly, I wish to offer myself as living proof that there is, without a doubt, freedom and joy even after such a terrible storm. Someone who was much wiser than me has already said it best. "The only thing needed for evil to prosper, is for good people to do nothing." Let's do something.

CHAPTER ONE

THE HAPPY YEARS

WHAT DOES A BASEMENT, A tractor shed and a crippled children's therapy clinic have in common? Tragically, they were all places where my brothers and sisters and I were routinely raped and molested as young children. Now just let me say before you roll your eyes that I already know how incredibly "worn out" that sounds. I can't help the seemingly endless line of ravenous child predators that never cease heaping their brand of bad news on us. And for the record, I don't really like hearing about it either. It's just that I'm beginning to fear that because of its insane frequency, we may be in real danger of succumbing to the sleepy hypnosis of its sick regularity. I mean honestly, day after day, we witness famous and regular people alike being hauled off to jail for all manner of sex crimes against children and though the parade of abuse never ends, it naturally tends to become a little less tragic with each hearing. So, since it's in our very nature to become desensitized, I have decided to shock your senses back into the fight and tell it all again. But this time I will venture to leave nothing out.

I guess the real question for me is; where does someone even begin to tell such a story as this? I mean, the practical side of me screams "Don't do it, man! No one wants to hear this stuff any more!" But having witnessed and experienced all that I have, my conscience presses me to type on. Who knows whether God may use my story to help another? But where do I begin? I suppose in this particular case, the beginning should appropriately coincide with my own uneventful beginning.

I was born in Kentucky in the spring of 1966, to a couple of young middleclass sweethearts. They were middle class only in so much as they themselves had been born to middle class parents. Like so many other young baby boomers around them, my parents simply joined the crowd, fit in and found themselves doing whatever felt good to them at the time. Caught in the same ignorant snare as many of their lusty young peers, they had become parents long before they could even begin to imagine another life. They were barely out of their teens and I was their second child.

Shortly after my birth, tragedy struck that young couple when my older brother John, at the age of eighteen months, contracted stomach cancer and passed away. Even now I cannot begin to imagine what those two went through as they suffered such a soul crushing loss. If their youthful lack of commitment wasn't already driving them apart, this certainly hurried things along. A year and a half later, my younger brother, (who in this story will be called Eli) was born and already the memories of my dad were becoming few and far between. By the time my sister (whom we shall call Sarah) was born in 1970, I remember saying goodbye to my dad for the last time. It would be more than ten years before I would see him again.

Most of my first four years were spent with my mother, as we lived with her parents. For me, these were the happy times. Our maternal grandparents genuinely loved and cared for me and Eli. But it was our paternal grandparents who truly doted on us. I do not have a single bad memory of any time spent with them. As a matter of fact, I don't have a single bad memory of that period of my young life except for the death of my Grandpa Kincer (my mom's dad). I was actually still pretty young when he passed away and I don't really remember much about him. I do remember his funeral though and all of the silly childish questions I asked. "Can he wake up?" "Can he move?" "What if he has an itch?" It's funny the things we remember.

My earliest memories of Grandma Kincer are of an old lady with white hair. She past away nearly twenty five years later and I never remember seeing her look any other way. Most of the time during those early years, we lived with her in Florence, Kentucky. She kind of took over the responsibility of helping to raise Eli and me, since mom had to work. Cepha Davis-Kincer was an extraordinary woman. She was tender and sweet, like all grandmothers should be, but had the back bone of ten men when she needed it. And believe me; with several young boys growing up under her roof, she needed it. She was a typical, faithful, middle class member of her local Presbyterian Church and she also happened to be my earliest teacher, instructor, encourager and disciplinarian. Every day, she bathed us, fed us, clothed us and oh how she loved us. In addition to her custodial duties, she would also regularly take me aside to the living room couch and read to me from her large, black leather bound Bible. I particularly enjoyed the pictures, which always came with liberal doses of her own insightful explanations. To this day, I carry the values that she taught me and to this day I have the very Bible from which she read to me in my collection. I will be forever indebted to her for the foundation on which my life has been built.

Jack and Evelyn Wischer, on the other hand, saw much less of us and spent most of their time spoiling Eli and me. Every waking moment with them was fun. Each morning at their home, I would rise early and find that they had already been awake for quite some time. They were just sitting out there sipping their coffee and waiting for their sleepy little prince to come out and join them. I would eventually make my entrance while rubbing the sleep from my eyes, to which they would explode with exaggerated cheers as though the President himself had just walked in. They would take turns holding me and kissing me good morning. Then Grandma would ask me the same question that she had asked me a thousand times before. "How much do I love you?" My response was as well rehearsed as her question, "A bushel and a peck and a hug around the neck?" Then she would grab me a squeeze me and say, "You bet your handsome neck I do!" I would then eat my breakfast with a big canary eating grin on my face while she busied herself applying her own war paint for the day. Grandpa, who was sitting on the other side of me, smoked his cigarette and read his paper. Every now and then, he would peek out from behind his great big wall of print to offer me a wink and a smile. Grandma, not wishing to be out done, would reach over, rub my head and ask me how my breakfast was. It was quite a little racket I had going there. Barely four years old and I owned both of them.

Grandpa and I would then bundle up and head out. It was our job to go out into the freezing cold and warm up that old white 1965 Scooby-Doo van of theirs, so that Grandma could come out to a warm ride. I guess back then the van wasn't so old. We would then drive her to the airport where she worked. I always sat between them on the warm engine cover, since the motor was mounted between the two front seats of those vans. While Grandpa navigated those winding country roads to the airport, Grandma and I would sing along with the AM radio to songs like, "Me and you and a dog named Boo." Grandpa endured those performances most patiently, offering his usual grin between each song. After delivering our passenger to the airport, Grandpa and I would bid her a good day with hugs and kisses and continue on our way, stopping only for gas and our daily Clark Bar and Lemon-Lime soda. Then it was off to their farm to work on their new house or maybe his tractor. Some days we didn't work at all. We would just go fishing in the pond that was on their land. I do not remember Grandpa ever denying me any of my childish whims or ever saying no to me and for his kindness I repaid him with copious amounts of grief as my boundless energy and reckless abandon found me constantly injuring myself at every opportunity. Yep, I was that kid. Once I fell from a narrow wooden plank which had been placed across a newly poured concrete sidewalk. The plank was only a foot or two above the walk but it seemed like a hundred feet to me. Back and forth I marched until one misplaced step brought me tumbling down. I was fortunate this time to have only received a small cut on my forehead. But given enough time, I could surely out do that one. Not long after that, I decided that Grandpa needed my "help" as he worked on his tractor. I picked up his claw hammer and began to wale on the large rear tire. I remember hearing him say something like "be careful with that thing please" just as the inevitable occurred. The hammer, which had bounced past my head five or ten time before, finally found its mark. The claw pinged me on my forehead just above my left eye and—bang! Lights out. I remember waking up in a wheel chair at a hospital surrounded by nurses who were kissing me on my head and checking my wound. Grandpa, who was my hero, had once again scooped me up and rushed me to this familiar place to once again, be patched up. Even these are great memories.

My mother was our best friend in those days. When she was not at work, she saw to it that she was with us, listening patiently to all the adventures of her two little boys, who had just spent the day driving their Grandmother bonkers. Then, probably in an effort to give Grandma a much needed break from us, we would take our evening walk down "Rocky Road" to the local drug store for some sweet tarts before returning home to watch *The Adventures of Superman*. She was now a single mom, who had recently lost one of her babies to cancer and who still had to work hard to pay our bills. Even with this incredible burden and painful loss, I never remember seeing it on her face or hearing it in her voice. She did a pretty good job of insolating us from all of that. I did not know it then, but these were going to be the happiest years of my childhood.

The Divorce

I can remember so little about my father in those days that I simply will not have much to say here. I honestly could not fill one hand with the number of appearances that he made in my life back then, at least any that I could remember. I just remember that my happy little world was suddenly invaded with some strange new tension and anger which seemed to come out of nowhere. I had no idea what it was all about, but I certainly knew that the people around me were not at all happy. Then came the day of drama at Grandpa Wischer's farm. I was just a little guy sitting outside the barn on Grandpa's tractor, watching the many private meetings that kept ending in loud arguments. It was after one of those arguments that my dad came out to me and said goodbye. He said it with conviction as though he was mad at someone, but I knew it wasn't me. That goodbye would be it for more than a decade. I have no memory of missing him or feeling sorry that he was leaving. He simply wasn't there anyway. Now if it had been my mother or grandparents saying goodbye, I would have had a meltdown.

As I mentioned earlier, my mom was now a single working mom, with two hungry boys to feed and another child on the way. We were living with her mother and I guess she knew that something was going to have to give sooner or later. About that time, she began to fall in love with her boss. This was a dreadful decision that would change everything forever.

The Happy Years End.

It was not long before mom was introducing us to her new flame from work. He was like no other person I had ever known. From the perspective of a four-year-old, he genuinely looked like an unhappy fellow who had a face to match his disposition. I was never happy to see him and always happy when he left. Of course I had no idea at age four, that this guy was a "flame" in my mom's eyes and I certainly had no idea that he was about to become a more permanent fixture in my happy little world. That happy little world was about to be assaulted in every way imaginable and there is certainly no way that a four year old could have seen that coming. I had simply become accustomed to going along for the ride and being loved at every turn. I was too young to fathom the possibility of such a subhuman evil dwelling among normal people.

The very next thing that I remember was mom moving us all into this man's home. For the sake of this story only, we will call him Devlin. He lived in Cincinnati, Ohio, on a little cul-de-sac not far from where my grandparents lived. My new sister Sarah, who had recently been born with a debilitating spinal disease and who was still in the hospital fighting for her young life, would not come home for the first time for many months. But when she did, it would be straight into the arms of evil.

CHAPTER TWO

BOYS, SAY HELLO TO YOUR NEW FATHER

ELI AND I WERE NEVER considered ill tempered children by any stretch of the imagination. We were, in point of fact very typical three and four year old boys. We always had family members close to us who loved us and who could also jerk the slack out of our cord when that was needed. But I guess Devlin did not carry those same affections for us. He obviously liked my mother since he had asked her to live with him. But it was immediately evident that he did not like me and Eli. We knew what it was like to be loved and this was anything but.

Devlin had two children of his own from a previous marriage whom we shall call Nathan and Rebecca. Nathan was a handsome three years old boy, while Rebecca was a gorgeous two year old little girl. Sarah had still not come home from the hospital yet, though she would soon. I was not yet five years old when we all became a family, and I was the oldest, which should give some indication as to how terribly young we all were when this whole mess began. I don't know if it was because we were so young or because of the tremendous amount of violence in the home, but for some reason all five of us children bonded pretty well, at least at first.

If you would have asked me as a four year old to describe Devlin in one word, I would have said *"Mean"*. It was painfully obvious that he did not care about me; in fact I don't think that he even cared much for his own children either. Any so-called parental discipline he implemented was far too mean-spirited and cruel to have achieved anything constructive. Instead, his angry outbursts at us only succeeded in forcing us to live in utter fear around him. The strange thing was that he never seemed to be ashamed to exhibit this cruel behavior in the presence of other family or even total strangers. No matter where we were, if our childish antics drew his attention, he would blurt out in front of God and everyone who was listening, "When we get home, I'm going to beat the mortal hell out of you!" What those bystanders did not know is that he meant it. Fifteen or twenty lashes with a leather belt to a three or four year old will get you jail time today and very likely the loss of your children. But that was a different time and this was his idea of discipline. Thus the stage was being set for what would be the worst decade of my life.

My son is four years old now. I often look at him and wonder what would possess someone my size to wale on him in a rage. He is a very normal four year old who already knows how to fully test the boundaries of his parent's patience. But to attack and destroy that childish zest for life and reduce him to a terrified prisoner, would be simply demonic. Now there are some very important things that my wife and I need our little boy to understand and simply obey. At times I have caught him testing my resolve in these matters and have had to do my parental business by taking him by his hand, looking into his eyes and reminding him of these very important rules. I then give him a couple of good stings on his fanny, which he does not soon forget. But then something extraordinary happens. Within minutes of that confrontation, he comes back into the living room and finds me sitting on my couch and watching the news, right where he left me. Then in his normal fashion, he climbs up next to me and then straight up my back, using my head as a balancing stone. He then stands straight up on my shoulders and yells, "Hey, mom, look at me." This drives his mother crazy. He then begins to jockey for my attention and attempts to seduce me into a round of "you can't catch me" or "hide and seek." He's not afraid of me; he simply hugs me and goes right back to being my little boy. This was never the case in Devlin's home. If he was there, we remained as quiet prisoners, trying to keep out of sight and below his radar. If he was not home, we lived in dreadful expectation of his return.

To reinforce his intimidation even if we were not misbehaving, he would employ bizarre tactics. For instance, while brushing my hair and for no apparent reason, he would often turn the brush over and give me a couple of good conks on the head. I mean good conks, the kind that would rattle my teeth. These were most effective because of the surprise factor. I never saw them coming. Then he would just look at me and smile. Well, what is a four year old going to do when you bash him on the head? I began to cry. Then the smirk would leave his face and would become that sober, angry glare. He would then demand "Dry up!" I knew full well what that meant. It meant stop crying or you will get a beating or as he would put it *"a real reason to cry"*. We learned right away to control and suppress our emotions. Believe it or not, this level of fear and physical abuse was achieved within the first few weeks of our arriving at his home. But things were about to take a turn for the horrific.

The real nightmare begins

Although we did not know it yet, the aforementioned abuses were only a precursor to the terrible things which were to come. Within the first month of living in Devlin's home, Eli and I had effectively been cut off from our beloved grandparents and other family and were literally being reduced to objects instead of little boys. I suppose that any psychologist worth his degree could tell you that these were all textbook behaviors of a child abuser. Isolate the victim and chop off the humanity. But what does a four year old know about all of that?

What happened next was entirely too graphic to be written. I'll just say that on that day, I became the victim of sexual abuse. Afterward he threatened to hurt me very badly if I ever told anyone. "Do you understand me?" he said. He then made me repeat those terrible words so that he would know that I understood. I was then dismissed and I retreated to a corner of the back yard to hide until everyone came home. This terrifying experience signaled a remarkable escalation in the abuse, which by no means diminished or halted the beatings and threats which continued as well.

I did not know it then, but later learned that Eli was on the receiving end of the same sexual abuse at the same time. Sarah, who was still a baby, was now home from the hospital. Mom had been told that she would never walk, but that would not prevent this slug from also targeting her and his own daughter Rebecca as well in the not so distant future.

This sexual abuse continued with me a number of times over the next few months. Each episode was always followed by the same physical abuse and terrible threat, after which I would run off to hide for a while. Then, just after my fifth birthday, the abuse dramatically escalated once again.

I was enrolled in the first grade at a local elementary school. The school was less than ten blocks from Devlin's house so I walked to and from. There was, ironically enough, a hill that I had to walk down and then back up to get there each day. And in the winter, if it snowed, well you know the rest. Anyway, it was on one of those afternoon walks home that it happened. As I slowly walked home daydreaming and counting the sidewalk joints as they went by, I heard a car horn honking behind me. It startled me and I turned quickly to see. I immediately recognized Devlin's angry bearded face behind the wheel as he was commanding me to get in. I love the way my son rejoices with a loud "Dad!" after not seeing me all day. But the opposite would occur when I would see Devlin. As usual, he did not say a word as he drove the few remaining blocks to his house. We went in and once again I discovered that we were alone. I fully expected to be summoned to the basement for another round of abuse, knocks on the head and threats of being harmed. But to my horror I was led back to his bedroom this time. He began to take off his clothes and instructed me to do the same. My terrified little mind was racing. What could he possibly want? Even with what had already happened to me, I was still too young and innocent to comprehend what was about to happen. Then the unthinkable happened. At the innocent age of five, I was raped for the first time by a true child predator. When it was over, he once again threatened to hurt me very badly if I told anyone what he had just done, but this time he added "and if you tell anyone I will kill your mommy and you will never see her again." That was the worst threat of them all. I wasn't sure if mom knew anything about all of this or not, but I was always sure that one day she would help me. The mere thought of losing her and being left alone with Devlin was too terrifying to even consider. I immediately began to have regular nightmares about my mom being run over by a steam roller. In those awful dreams I would cry so hard, that I would literally wake myself up. After he said that to me, I just stood there, all three foot nothing of me, in so much physical pain that even trying to answer him knocked the breath out of me. He dismissed me and again I retreated. The pain was too much to even walk, so I never made it outside this time. I just sat on a soft chair in the living room and stared out the window. I just sat there silently for the rest of the day, choking back tears for fear of losing my mother. I just wished so desperately at that moment that I was back at

Grandpa's farm with him. Such thoughts kept my mind off the pain and perhaps kept me from losing my mind altogether.

This scene was repeated a number of times while we lived there in Cincinnati. The same was already happening to Eli as well and although we did not know it at that time, this was only the beginning of what would become a ten year nightmare for us and our siblings.

Let me just add that it was also the beginning of a nightmare for our mother as well. From the very beginning we had a front row seat to the physical violence that afflicted her as well. We could only listen to the sounds of our mommy being beaten and her screams for help. She had to hide the bruises the same as we did. She was young and also cut off from her family and very much afraid of this ruthless man. For these notable reasons, I never felt inclined to blame her or hold her accountable for what Devlin alone was responsible. To this very day our mother is still very close to most of her children and now her grandchildren. For the past twenty five years, she has tirelessly attempted to say that she was sorry for something that she did not do. I have assured her that there is nothing to forgive and that she should be happy and move on. But back then the nightmare was just beginning for all of us.

A child's soul begins to die

It is a terribly unnatural thing to force a child from his carefree innocent life into a rugged full time mode of survival. But this is exactly what was happening to us. As you can imagine my family life had become a sick, twisted mess. My outside social skills were nonexistent and my education was always suffering because there was simply no life energy left when I was at school. It had all been sapped out of me during the carnage at home.

Just then perhaps the most awful thing happened to me. My Grandma and Grandpa Wischer, who were neither stupid nor blind and after having been cut off from us for quite some time, located Devlin's house and paid us a surprise visit. When I first walked into the room and saw them, my heart leapt for joy. I knew they would come, I just knew it. Maybe they will take us home with them and rescue us. Devlin, who was more surprised by their visit than any of us and for good reason, was also standing in the room guarding his prey. With a stern clearing of his throat we looked at him and realized that we were miles from any rescue. From that moment on, we said nothing to them unless we were asked. They looked so helpless sitting there staring at us. I remember seeing them turn to each other and saying out loud, "These aren't our boys. Something is happening to them." We just stood there like two zombies while they tried their best to interrogate Devlin. He cleverly put on a sheepish face, one that I had never seen before and responded, "I'm sorry; I have no idea what you're talking about. These boys are fine." As they exhausted their arguments, it dawned on me that they were preparing to leave and that I would not be going with them. I wanted to cry and scream out for help, but genuinely feared that he would kill my mom if I did. So I just stood there, never taking my eyes off of them, not even for a moment. I wanted to hug them and sit on their lap, but I was paralyzed. The visit ended with them giving us a few toys and a Sesame street record album. They then kissed us and told us that they loved us very much. As I watched them leave, my soul literally began to die. All of my hope had rested on the dream that they would one day come and save me. When that dream vaporized in front of me, I had nothing left to look forward to except the very blackness of hell—and I was only five years old.

Their visit must have frightened Devlin, because he suddenly felt the need to move. In no time at all, we had packed a U-haul truck and headed south. Yep, just like that, all the way to New Orleans, Louisiana. I was too young to understand the geography, but I remember how long we were on the road and I somehow knew that every tree or sign or bridge that went by meant that I was getting farther and farther away from my Grandparents. It would, in fact, be nearly five years before I would see or hear from them again. I was simply going to have to learn to cope with my new prison and would have to do so without them. I know now that our move was no ordinary move. We were definitely on the run. That visit was a close call, depending on your perspective and that was a loose end that needed to be taken care of.

We did not live there in New Orleans very long, a few months maybe. I know this because I was enrolled into the second grade while we lived there and I never finished. I had to continue the second grade in our next location. Devlin must have been really shaken because none of us can remember any sexual abuse during those months in Louisiana. But it was not long until we were on the move again. This time we landed in Hancock County, Mississippi. There we moved into a tiny logging town called Kiln, on the southern tip of the state, near the gulf coast. You can't even begin to imagine how small and hidden away from my family that town was. No one would ever find us or pay us any surprise visits there. Once we arrived, the abuse resumed in earnest.

CHAPTER THREE

YEAR AFTER YEAR NO HELP IN SIGHT

DEVLIN WAS A GENIUS IN his own mind and he really knew how to play the part. Now it doesn't take a genius to find a simple-minded man and take advantage of him. But Devlin, who clearly had no conscience, had a bad habit of doing just that and was making a fairly good living at it as well. He was also a philosophical egocentric who wielded a better than average command of the English language. Wherever he lived, he cleverly exploited these lesser virtues to his full advantage; In other words, he knew how to make the neighbors like him and he would do so with a grace that belied his true nature. He was no Jekyll and Hyde--he simply knew how to conceal his criminal acts behind what appeared to be an equal measure of good citizenship. For instance, during the early days in southern Mississippi, he spent a considerable amount of time raising money to build a therapy center for crippled children in that area. It turned out that the center was quite a success and this instantly endeared him to the community. This in turn gave him the confidence to actually run for public office as a county commissioner. Devlin was a short fellow compared to most men and his ridiculous campaign slogan, which rather revealed his true colors, was "elect Devlin, the little man with the big surprise." Unbelievable! This pervert actually believed that he could sell anything, including himself, if he attached a sexual innuendo to it. It was really no wonder that even though he was widely respected as a local philanthropist "want to be," he was defeated in that race. But he always had his hands into something in those days. A lot of people still remember him down there to this very day. I know this because I returned to that small town for a visit in 1996, nearly twenty years after we had moved away and they were still asking about him and my mother by name.

One glance at his numerous pairs of elevator shoes and large automobiles and it was immediately evident that he was not at all comfortable with his physical stature. But he was still able to perform well enough in public as not to attract any negative attention to himself. No, if you wanted to observe the brutality that was occurring to us children, then watching Devlin was definitely not the way to go about it. **But by watching and observing the children** who lived in his home, one would not have to spend very much time at all before knowing that something was dreadfully wrong. We were exactly like that kidnapped little boy mentioned in the premise. We went to school every day; we had friends; we played several years of little league baseball--and yet we remained too terrified to simply ask for help.

Devlin's confidence in our fear also grew as time went by. For a fellow who fancied himself a genius, how could he not know that I was going to grow up one day? Nowadays, I regularly witness what seem to be an endless line of other men and women in the news revealing that someone had abused them when they were children. Honestly, what is wrong with these child abusing morons? Can they not see the future reckoning coming at them like a freight train? I suppose not.

The house that we lived in was old even by 1970 standards. But in those days it was considered sturdy, even "hurricane proof." It was constructed of heavy lumber and was elevated about three feet above the ground. It was lass than a hundred yards from the Jordan River, which made possible the local logging industry. I suppose that the three foot elevation was considered flood protection. By today's standards, this house never would have been built, but strangely enough, she did successfully withstand hurricanes Betsy, Carmen and Cameal and probably others that I don't know about. So who knows? Anyway, the old girl stood there like an oak on nearly ten acres of property which backed up to a large pine forest. The house sat at a point farthest away from that forest, while the new therapy center sat on the opposite side of the property right next to the wood line. There was a large, two-stall garage which was separated from the house by fifty feet or so. These unattached garages were all over that town in those days and no one seemed to be using them for any thing as frivolous as parking their car. It appeared that their primary use was for sheltering one's tractor and farming tools, which were of far greater value than any family car. With Devlin's pack-rat nature, both of these rooms were full in no time and with pure rubbish, of which he would never have need or use of. A hundred yards in the opposite direction of the river from the house, was a small Catholic school. Behind it was a large field with play ground equipment and several baseball diamonds. This new rural setting offered a wonderful new world of play-time exploration for a boy my age, but it also offered a terrible plethora of new hiding places for Devlin to extract his sick pleasure at our expense.

For a community which appeared (from my perspective) to be mostly elderly, there was no shortage of children. Although I have no first hand knowledge of any of these children, some of whom were my friends, ever being victimized by Devlin, I have always felt certain that some were. I now know that true child predators usually leave numerous victims over a span of many years. In other words, there were probably victims before Devlin ever met me and there were probably victims long after I was gone. With staggering numbers like that, I'm convinced that other children in that town had fallen victim to him as well.

Now our childhood nightmare was in no way a reflection of this little town at all. On the contrary, it really was a beautiful place. The experience was much more than simply a move south. It was like landing fifty years in the past as well. The center of town was a cross- road with the town's only traffic light. It was, in fact, a single blinking light which saw very little traffic. Half a mile from our house was a small, old-time general store, which looked as though it had been plucked from the set of *The Waltons*, cast and all. For anything resembling a modern grocery store, we would have to leave town and drive all the way to Bay Saint Louis. Our Sheriff's name was Sylvan Ladner. I do not remember much about the man himself, but I do remember that he drove a patrol car that resembled Sheriff Andy Griffith's from Mayberry. I don't remember any deputies in those days either, but it may be that I just never saw them. There were only two churches in town that I can remember. One was the Catholic Church; the other was the Shifalo Baptist Church, where I publicly became a believer. The people in that town were kind people who seemed to do more than simply tolerate children. They were genuinely fond of them. Even those tough old log truck drivers liked us. They drove those giant rigs right past our house numerous times every day. Over time we knew them all by face. With the old string pulling motion of our hands as they rolled by, they would never fail to offer us a big smile and a short blast of their air horn. That never got old. Now it was a strict standing rule that no children were allowed at the log yard. There were simply too many trucks and large machines zooming about. But almost daily, that is precisely where you could find us, climbing those endless piles of logs or fishing from the barges which were waiting to be loaded with lumber. I suppose the workers knew that we were there and just pretended not to see us as they carefully maneuvered around us. They would ignore us until one of us would catch a fish and then--well, let me just say that I have never seen anyone with enough will power to ignore a fish being caught. Instantly several men would rush over to get a closer look at our trophy as it flopped about on the river bank. There was always a brief conversation about the bait that was used and the location of the catch. That was usually followed by the telling of a few of their own fish stories. Then, with some hardy laughs and congratulatory pats on the back, they would hurry back to their posts. For the most part they seemed like a great group of guys. Our neighbor also seemed to genuinely like us. He never seemed to mind if we snuck into his yard and picked a few pears from his tree. That place had such potential for being a truly wonderful place for a boy to grow up. It is a travesty that it was instead a place where my worst nightmares came true.

It was the early 1970s, and children's public television and top forty R and B radio ruled the day. It would be years before we would see our first video game or any thing like cable television. Besides, who wanted to be inside? There were simply too many forts to be built, or fish to be caught, or football games to be played. There were trees to be climbed and frogs to capture. Outside was a world of excitement just waiting to be discovered. My brothers and I owned Crossman pellet rifles, which also provided endless hours of excitement. In our eight year old vast reservoirs of wisdom, we had convinced each other that if we shot any wild animal in the head with our trusty pellet rifle, that animal would surely die. One day we lit out after a wild hog that had ventured near our land. I know that we shot that hog fifteen or twenty times about the head and shoulders with those pellet guns and only succeeded in making the animal angry. We did not know it then, but we were very fortunate that he did not decide to turn on us. That episode required us to rethink the power of our weaponry. But we never gave a second thought to the wisdom of the actual chase itself. "We'll get him next time" was our motto.

Our school was the only one that I knew about in that county, other than the smaller Catholic school. Hancock North Central School offered first through twelfth grades all on one campus, at least back then. I arrived in the middle of second grade and spent the remainder of that year under the tutelage of Mrs. Bounze. Now it has been more than thirty years since I studied there and am very likely butchering the spelling of these names. I can only pray that these fine educators will forgive the years that have stolen some of my memory. I moved on to the third grade with Mrs. House, followed by the fourth grade with Mrs. A. Ladner, Mrs. M. Ladner and Mr. Detoe. Fifth grade was spent with Mrs. Gray and, finally, it was on to the sixth grade with another Mrs. Ladner. We moved again nearly half way through the sixth grade school year, but not before I made a few lasting memories there.

Now I wasn't very good at basketball and I wasn't allowed to join the football team, but five years of Little League baseball afforded me five long seasons of unforgettable boyhood pleasure. I will never forget the magic of how the uniforms, the cheering parents and the smell of roasting hamburgers and hotdogs all meant that we would be spending the afternoon in heaven. I mean really, what could possibly be better at that age? We had dozens of grown ups applauding us all day long, while all the littler kids were worshiping us as heroes as we majestically pranced about in our game day best. And, of course, don't forget about the girls; all those pretty girls who kept checking us out as though some lofty celebrities had just blown into town. Ah yes, good times indeed. Of course, once the uniforms were sent to the laundry, all of those super powers quickly vanished away, immediately returning us to our miserable obscurity. But there was always next Saturday.

Meanwhile, back at school I was becoming quite a marble shooter in my own right and was quickly amassing a sock full of those little glass balls that we boys treasured so dearly. I proudly displayed them by tying that sock to one of my side belt loops so that all could view my victories. I can still hear them rattling around in there as I walked about the playground searching for my next contest. I know how corny that all sounds now, but believe me, back then it was quite possibly the most significant indicator, at least to our pre-teenaged peers, of our emerging manhood. Very important stuff indeed. John Peter Garcia was my best buddy in those days. He had given me one of his marbles as kind of a starter gift and in no time I owned half the marbles in our class, including many of his.

These were indeed much simpler times. It would be nearly fifteen years before we would see personal computers in people's homes and almost twenty before we would see people walking around with cell phones stuck to their ears. Eight-track tapes and Converse tennis shoes were all the rage. There was simply no reason for a young boy to waste much time in the house. As far as I was concerned, the inside of the house was only a hellish place where terrible things happened to me. But outside were many short furloughs and distractions from those troubling realities within. I became a master at taking advantage of such distractions by completely immersing myself into every adventure that came my way.

For example, consider the numerous animals that we owned in those days. On any given day, one could easily find half a dozen dogs and cats running unfettered about our property. We also owned a couple of horses and three cows. One of those cows was actually a cantankerous young bull, whom we affectionately named Meany Marvin. This animal earned his name with his contrary disposition, in that he absolutely did not appreciate or find any amusement with little boys being in his field. This was not good for me, since it was in fact my job to regularly go into that field and feed him. Every day, if you wished, you could witness the same hilarious drama as it unfolded at feeding time. It was way better than any spy thriller on television, that's for sure. First you would watch as our young hero very stealthily entered the field as to remain undetected by the villainous Meany Marvin. But each day the young lad would discover, as he had discovered every day prior, that Marvin was always watching and merely awaiting the opportunity to spring his trap. Unfortunately for our hero, Marvin's feeding area was in the center of the field under a large pecan tree. Whoever designated that tree as the feeding spot should be prosecuted. Slowly and gently, the boy made his way toward that tree laden with an iron kettle of feed, which was a full quarter of his own weight. Meanwhile, that bull would just stand there a little ways off eating grass and pretending not to concern himself with the boy at all until he would get close to the tree and far away from the fence. Then, suddenly and without pretence, the chase was on! As I fled for my ever-loving life, I could hear my mother from our back yard laughing hysterically and offering her unsolicited advice. "Drop the food," she would shout while trying to catch her breath, "He just wants the food." But I knew better. I had many times in the past tried that very tactic and discovered each time that it was not the food that he wanted, but rather me--the slippery little mouse who kept eluding his capture. I was beginning to get a sense that the contest had become personal for him. I would, as I had done so many times before, drop the food while still in a full run, leaving it between me and him. I would then utter a short prayer that he would stop and eat, only to glance back and see that determined look on his stupid face as he once again bypassed the food and closed in for the kill. I could hear the breath bursting out of his snout and I could feel the ground rumbling under his nimble hoofs as we both drew closer and closer to the barbed wire which would once again be my salvation. Everything was reduced to slow motion as my certain death was only moments away. Finally, out of a sheer love for life--namely my own--I would drop to the ground like a Navy Seal, rolling under the bottom wire to safety. Man that was close! I would then stand up tall and turn to face my nemesis. We were now standing face to face, only three feet apart with nothing between us but a few strings of wire. We both just stood there and glared at one another as we each tried to catch our breath. Now I have never seen emotion on a bull's face before, but I swear that Marvin looked furious. If he could have spoken, I know he would have said "I'll get you tomorrow, you little punk." What a mean animal. I mean, really, I was only trying to feed him. Well, he never did catch me. In fact we ate him the following spring. It served him right.

These glorious adventures served only as mild distractions to dull the mind numbing reality of the regular abuse at home. Any attempt on my part to cast the illusion of being a normal child was always undone by the deep running dysfunctions which continually vexed me. The truth was I was no normal child at all. I never felt safe. I was afraid of everyone and possessed no real self confidence of any kind. I couldn't even look an adult in the eye. Nothing ever made me feel secure and I had long forgotten what it felt like to be truly happy. My soul resembled an emaciated death camp prisoner, who had utterly been starved of life. The real shame is that I carried these dysfunctions well into my adult life and will, of course, never recover those years.

We lived there in Kiln, Mississippi for approximately five years and the sheer number of times that Devlin abused me sexually was staggering. This could occur in the garage or in the new therapy center after hours or in the house if we were again left alone. Many times after he had finished having his way with me and prior to issuing the regular barrage of threats, this twisted fellow would actually ask me if I liked it. Did I like it? Had he completely lost his mind? Or was he just getting off by provoking my anger and watching me have to hold it in? At that moment, my soul would cringe and my blood would boil. I wanted to explode with the rage of a mad man, but, I was still so small. My mind was bursting with pain and I so desperately desired at that very moment to hold it in no longer, but instead to thrust a blade into his heart, spit in his face and force him to hear just how much I hated it as he gasped for his final few breaths. When my wandering mind would finally snap back to the present, I would again be remorse to find him still very much alive and awaiting my response. I was certain that if I said no, I would be raped or beaten in retribution. So I learned to always say what I thought he wanted to hear. Thus my soul died a little more. He knew very well that I hated it---and him, for that matter. But continually breaking me down on the inside was just one more thing that brought him pleasure.

I was ten years old the last time that Devlin attempted to rape me. It occurred one night when my mother had gone out for the evening. I do not know where she went, but I immediately expected the worst. I put my baby brother Carson, who had just been born the previous year, on my bed so that he could sleep with me. I thought that maybe this would make Devlin leave me alone. My other plan was to hurry up and sleep through my mother's absence. I drifted off to sleep with a short prayer that God would hasten the arrival of the morning and with it the benevolent sound of my mother's voice from the next room. It seemed as though I had just fallen asleep when I was abruptly awakened by Devlin's knuckles banging on my head as though he were knocking on a door. I was still a small boy and was very groggy after being suddenly awakened. I remember saying something stupid like "I have to watch Carson" in an attempt to brush him off. But he simply knocked on my head that much harder. I then fully woke up and began to realize what was happening. With that same angry look, he motioned with a jerk of his finger as not to awaken my brothers and sisters. I'm certain that some of them lay there terrified; knowing very well what was about to happen to me. He then took me into another room and once again attempted to assault me. I decided that he would not succeed this time without a fight. I reasoned that any beating afterwards would be far less painful than the actual rape. This all may sound courageous, but it did not prevent my legs from trembling or the tears from falling. Then, as you can very well imagine, he attacked, and I mounted my fierce defense. I was able to keep up my resistance for a while, but unfortunately sustained several injuries during the incident. I actually have to see the scars of those injuries every day. At times they infuriate me, but mostly they remind me that there are still children out there who are being hurt, and need my help. As I continued to fight, he became increasingly frustrated. I suppose this ended the mood for him, because he pulled me to my feet, by the hair of my head and commanded "Go to bed!" Hallelujah! It worked! And I was right. I would take that beating any day over being raped.

It's a sad reality, but these were the days when a father should have been teaching his son how to become a man. I should have been learning about the glorious differences between the sexes and what a wife would need from a husband one day or, for that matter, what I would need to be looking for in a wife. I should have been learning the truest definitions of love--how to love what is good and hate evil. I should have been learning how to stand and be strong in the face of adversity. I should have been learning about my future and how I should have been preparing for its arrival. But instead, I was learning the very antithesis of these virtues. Although I have made slow and steady progress in my recovery, these deficits stunted my development for years to come. But God is good and as He had never abandoned me during those darkest of hours, so He has not forsaken me in my journey to health.

CHAPTER FOUR

CARNAL KNOWLEDGE

I'M A LITTLE APPREHENSIVE ABOUT telling this next part, but the truth is, I am a fairly good example of what can happen to a boy who is brought up in a world where sex is a punch line. I've kept this little secret hidden away for years and even now I'm having second thoughts about telling it. Oh well, here's to keeping it real.

I never told anyone about this until recently because it was just such an awful source of embarrassment for me. Even when I occasionally found the strength to beat back the humiliation for a moment or two, I was never really sure that telling it would even help anyone. So I guess it was just easier to keep it to myself. You know what I mean? Some things are just better left unsaid.

Anyway, not long ago I finally drew up enough courage to discuss it with a couple of friends. They were kind and after leaving me with their wisdom on the matter, I conclude that it would be better told than not.

One of the friends whom I laid this burden on was a Mr. Tim DeForest. Tim is himself an accomplished author and is also a pretty smart guy concerning the proper use of the Queen's English. It was Mr. DeForest who greatly assisted me with much of the sentence and paragraph structure in this little book and for that I thank him. He's a genuinely humble man and would never tell you this himself, but he also heroically removed around a million misused commas from my work as well. After receiving his scholarly reprimand it became clear that he held some inordinate hatred for commas and I fear that my liberal usage had actually kept him up nights. I am convinced that my dear brother only found peace again after having dashed every last one from existence with his mighty pen. And for that we all thank him. Humor aside, it was Tim and another dear friend, whom I will mention in later chapters, who convinced me that there were indeed people who needed to hear this. So here it is.

One of the worst distortions of reality to plague me while I was growing up was my developing view of women. Every boy grows up developing some view of the fairer sex. Their outcome, however good or bad will be determined by what is or is not taught to them during those tender growing up years; as clearly demonstrated in this example of mine. My view of females had been meticulously twisted into knots by all that had happened to me. An unintended consequence, I'm sure, but a consequence nonetheless.

It all began to go aerie while I was still quite young. Sex was everywhere in my life. Aside from all of the sex that was actually happening to me, it was also laying around in every filthy magazine that Devlin owned. It was on television, in the movies and even on the radio, if you can believe that. I mean it was everywhere, just like today. Sex was always made sport of in front of the children and was never taught in any appropriate context. I was taught sex in every wrong way imaginable, and the rest was left for me to figure out for myself. So I did. At the age of five, I began to figure sex out for myself, and here's what I came up with.

It was clear to me, even at an early age, that men and women were doing many of the same things together, that Devlin was constantly doing to me, and this troubled me. Why would women volunteer for something like that? Didn't they know what was about to happen to them? Didn't they know how painful it was? Every time I saw a woman disappear into a bedroom with a man, I wanted to shout out to her "Don't go in there you fool! He's going to hurt you!" I heard the sounds that were coming out of those rooms also, whether on television or in real life, and truly believed that my worst fears for her were coming true (I was five). But they just kept going in there. What was wrong with them? Were women just stupid? Were they just stupid, easy targets like children? Unfortunately, this became my sincere conclusion for many years and would only worsen as I approached puberty.

As a young child I felt genuinely sorry for these stupid women. I regarded them as victims, much as I regarded myself. But as a teenager, I began to desire them. The tragedy only intensified when they began to desire me back. At that very moment, my pity turned to absolute distain for these stupid creatures. The fires had begun to burn in me and there was no hiding what I wanted from them. But what in the world could they have possibly wanted from me? Did they just want to be hurt? Well it was too late now, and I no longer cared. I knew what I wanted and if they were stupid enough to give it to me instead of running away from me, then they deserved to be hurt. Don't misunderstand me here. I wasn't running around looking for women to harm, but when it came to sex, I just didn't care if they enjoyed it or not. I was convinced that these dumb girls must have been placed here by God to pleasure men and not much else. I wasn't trying to hurt them; I just knew from long experience that it would hurt them. But they just never seemed to get it.

Don't ever try to tell me that teaching your sons about sex isn't important. Can you even imagine giving your daughter to a jerk like that? Well, be careful dads. There are literally tens of thousands of us out there with this warped since of reality who have no idea how precious your little girl really is. If you care at all for your daughters, then it is incumbent upon you to get to know the guy that she wants to be with. Don't be shy. Ask the hard questions. You may be saving your little girl from a world of hurt.

I'm incredibly thankful to God that I did not forever maintain this horrible view of women, but sadly it would be some years before I began to learn the truth about them. I know how dumb this must sound to someone who has never had the misfortune of enduring this particular problem, but you would faint to know just how large a problem this really is.

It took a long time, but by God's mercy I finally came to know just how beautiful and valuable women were in this universe of ours. They were made in His image just as I had been. Their bodies had been masterfully designed in the mind of their Creator to be nurtured, protected and loved by their husbands. They had been perfectly formed to both pleasure and to be pleasured sexually, and at no time did God ever intend for them to be harmed by some ignorant, selfish meat head who was blind to their true value.

The good news is that there is always hope. I am living proof that even a boy, whose view of women was polluted, can be healed.

CHAPTER FIVE

A FIRST FLIGHT TO FREEDOM

Any way, getting back to our journey, it was about that time that my mother and Devlin had some kind of falling out. It was very different from any of their normal arguments, which usually ended with Devlin hurting someone. This one was eerily quiet with a looming air of uncertainty. We all just walked around on egg shells for the next few days. This strange new silence seemed to terrorize us every bit as much and maybe even more than the more frequent explosive outbursts. At least we knew what was coming with those. But this creepy communication vacuum just kept us guessing. Finally, a few days later the silence was broken. Mom announced that she was leaving Devlin and that she would be taking me, Eli, Sarah and Carson. Nathan and Rebecca would be staying with their father. I could not believe it. We were finally getting out of there. I felt sorry for Nathan and Rebecca, but I was only ten years old and couldn't even save myself. It killed me to know that they were being left behind with that monster, because I knew very well what was going to be happening to them in our absence. It would probably be even worse for them considering that Devlin's victim pool had just shrunk by 75%. Nevertheless, within a few days I was saying goodbye to my younger brother and sister, whom I loved very much. We then boarded an airplane in Gulf Port, Mississippi and flew to Florence, Kentucky. I only recently discovered that Devlin had injured mom again and that was the reason we were leaving. He had thrown her to the ground and kicked her, leaving a horrendous bruise. One of Devlin's brothers and sister in law were visiting at the time giving my mother the courage to leave him. I did not know any of that at the time, but I didn't care. I was back at Grandma Kincer's house and happy to be there. It was not long before Grandma and Grandpa Wischer found out about our arrival and also came calling. We were definitely not the same boys that they had kissed goodbye some five years earlier; now all scruffy and frightened. But they were no less happy to see us. Soon we were riding around on that same old tractor and fishing in that same old pond as though we had never been gone. But we had indeed been gone and those five years were simply lost just as our childhood itself was lost. For now, though, none of that mattered as we spent every minute eagerly reconnecting with all of the family from whom we had been cut off for so long. I felt like the wealthiest and most liberated kid in the world. I really didn't know what to do with myself.

I think that I was basking in this new freedom for nearly a month when my mom abruptly announced that she was going to return to Devlin. What! You have got to be kidding me! Of course, she was not, nor was she interested in entertaining the opinion of her ten-year-old son. I just happened to be there when she said it and, anyway, who cares what a ten-year-old thinks. Who indeed? I could not believe what I was hearing. My mind convulsed. I felt like an invisible boy who had no voice. I felt as though I had just been dropped into the ocean a thousand miles from land with no one around to see me or hear me or save me. When it was apparent that I could do nothing to prevent this terrible reverse in fortune, I simply gave up and sank to the bottom. With amazing ease, I redressed my soul with those familiar rags of my poverty and accepted my doom. I know now that it was just my brain's way of bracing itself for the coming attack and, believe me, it was correct in doing so. To this day, I don't know what she was thinking or why she returned. Maybe it was because none of our family knew about the abuse and may have pressured her to reconcile. Whatever the reason, it was settled. And I was once again saying goodbye to the people I loved and returning to my prison. I know that at that moment I should have been screaming for help. But I had long come to believe that Devlin would make good on his promise to kill my mom. Children believe what the adults in their life tell them. If they receive the same threats year after year without end, then the threats become their reality. Their survival utterly depends on believing them. I had lived with

Devlin for years and witnessed first hand what he was capable of. So I kept my mouth shut.

Upon arriving back in Southern Mississippi, Devlin immediately seized the opportunity to find out if his secret was still safe. I guess he felt safe enough because the sexual assaults resumed immediately, as did the beatings and the threats. I did miss Nathan and Rebecca immensely and, although I hated returning, my reunion with them did help to ease the pain.

About that time, Devlin enrolled himself in some college classes that were far out of town. As a matter of fact, in order for him to attend, he needed to remain at the school all week long only returning home for the weekends. This lasted for most of the following year, which afforded me numerous week long vacations from my tormentor. The freedom was nearly as fantastic as being back in Kentucky. In fact, it was freedom on every level. You see, Devlin not only found enjoyment in molesting and beating children, but he also hated to see us enjoying ourselves. Watching television or playing was considered a waste of time. He thought that it was time better spent working with him in the garden or on any other of his numerous projects. Our friends, who often invited us to come and play, would constantly be answered with the same five infamous words: "No, we have to work." Devlin's absence brought something of an end to this play-time prohibition and we were again free to be kids. My mother loved to see us play and laugh and act like kids. Right after Devlin would leave she would unlock all of those dark prison gates and tear down all those dreaded barriers which had so successfully kept us from celebrating our childhood. Like young horses let out to pasture, we ran out kicking and bucking in all directions. I visited my friends in those days more than ever before. I climbed more trees, I played more football and the fishing—oh, and the fishing was fantastic. Every day I would exit the school bus two blocks from our house and run all the way home. I would yell to my mom as I entered the yard to announce my arrival and my departure. I slung my books toward the front porch and ran to the garage, where my fishing pole and tackle box had been dutifully waiting for me all day. I would scoop them up and run like the wind to the river bank to find my "happy place." There you could find me sitting, most days, well past dark and would only scamper home when mom came to find me.

Now all of this meant that we only had to tolerate Devlin for the two days that he was home from school. We even found ways to escape having to be with him during that time as well. For instance, my mom was fond of going to church and Devlin hated it. Every time she went, I went. Most kids I knew didn't like going to church at all because it took away from their weekend play-time. I was different. I would have gladly gone to get a tooth pulled if it meant getting away from Devlin for a while. Therefore, I was never forced to go to church. In fact, I rather liked it. I was never preoccupied with the frustration of not wanting to be there and, believe it or not. I actually got the message. At age nine, all of the things that Grandma Kincer had taught me about the Savior when I was a toddler were coming back to me. Jesus was becoming more than a story book character. I was beginning to see the Son of God as a real person. He was really alive and was not at all hiding himself from me. He was actually revealing himself to me in so many ways. As I learned the Bible, I was beginning to see the reason for it all. I was beginning to understand just how dearly God really loved me. I had no idea why he loved me, but, man, I could feel it. The fact that he had sent his only Son to die on a Roman cross for *my* guilt, to make *me* righteous, was literally reaching out across the ages and speaking volumes to me. Now I know that's all a bit puzzling to some folks. I mean, really, I've had this same discussion many times over the years as people scratch their heads and ponder the deeper theological problem that my testimony presents to them. Although I could never have produced an acceptable answer to them back then, the riddle has always remained the same. Why wasn't Jim angry at God for the brutality that he was being forced to endure? That's a fair question. The truth is I really can't remember why I wasn't angry at him. It really was a long time ago. Looking back on it now, I think I was just too young then to have surmounted or even entertained such deep theological arguments. My reality at age nine was simple. I knew very well who it was that was hurting me and it certainly wasn't God. I simply never blamed him for the terrible things that Devlin alone was guilty of and if you can believe this, he often rescued me from some of those terrible things before they even had a chance to occur.

For instance, many times, when I knew that something terrible was about to happen, I would pray for help and just like that some person would just show up out of the blue and interrupt the impending attack before it occurred. Or sometimes after praying Devlin's rage would simply evaporate right before my eyes and he would just decide not to beat me. These were true miracles for a severely abused little boy and absolute proof that God was actually concerned for me and was working on my behalf. I never knew why he allowed me to go through this awful mess. I don't think that I ever gave it much thought. I do know that I never felt inclined to shake my fist at the Creator of the universe and demand answers. I didn't know how he had made the sun and the moon, or how he made this world and every perfect beautiful living thing in it. But I did know, given the former, that he was not a mere man to be argued with or dismissed out of hand. I also knew that he was there with me and that he was as real to me as anything in this broken down world ever was. I guess I really don't know a simpler way to say it except that when God arrives to live inside of you, his presence absolutely can not be denied. The universe itself cannot contain him, yet there he was inside such a little one as me. Fantastic when you think about it; and he brought with him a love and a peace that this world had never been able to give to me. When I considered Jesus hanging up there on that piece of wood in my defense and for my sins, I never doubted his love for me again. It is truly an awesome thing to hear God speak your name, telling you that he is your truest Father; that he loves you; and that you are safe. I know. I can already hear the deep sigh of some one wishing to inquire, "Safe! You call that safe? You didn't sound very safe to me!" I get it, but safe is really rather subjective, isn't it? I mean, it's completely relative to the user's situation. In my case, it was God who was saying it to me. Even then, from my bottom of the pit perspective, I knew exactly what that meant. It meant that no matter what this life was throwing at me, nothing would ever be able to take away the *eternal life* that his Son had purchased for me. I was safe indeed and no one would ever be able to separate me from his love. I did ask him numerous times to remove me from this hellish existence and in looking back, I see now his answer was always yes, but I would just have to wait a little while longer. I have found this to be his usual answer to me down through the years. I'm fine with that. For most of my life now, I have rested comfortably in the knowledge that when my brief journey here is finished, I will open my eyes on the other side and see his face and know that I am truly home.

Well, when those Sunday services were over, mom would typically go grocery shopping at the A&P with the meager funds that Devlin had thrown her way. While she was busy stretching those dollars to feed us for that next week, I was next door at the TG&Y, buying plastic worms and jigs with my spare change. Devlin kept us pretty poor, but mom always found some money to share with me. After that, it was back home to face the hater. I never told anyone, but I prayed a thousand times for his death. What a terrible thing for a child to feel the need to wish for. It was a prayer that was strangely answered some thirty-five years later. It would, in fact, be many years before I would learn the awesome power of forgiveness. I will elaborate on this particular power in a later chapter.

Devlin must have been taking college classes in order to land a civil service job, because when he had finished school we moved again. This time we landed in Columbus, Mississippi, which was a much larger town than Kiln. Devlin went to work for the Social Security Office at the federal building and once again we had to finish a school year at a new school. But this time things were different.

A room full of second graders will receive a new member into their class with loving kindness, but sixth graders, not so much. Due to my dark, personal secret and my lack of any companionship at this new place, I sank into a general state of disinterest. I wasn't lazy; I just didn't have anyone to impress. By the end of the school year, I had failed every subject and had to repeat the sixth grade. This was a new low for me and it marked the beginning of a scholastic roller coaster ride that would last until my senior year. The season of Devlin being gone all week was over and it was business as usual. He was now home from work every evening at 5:30 and eager to make life intolerable. I was miserable at school and I was miserable at home. I was defeated and I knew it. I was now eleven years old and was still being sexually abused by Devlin every time he thought that he could get away with it.

I suppose that I was now old enough to receive a new and more effective threat. The threats of mutilation and of killing my mother were now being preceded by a direct threat that I too would be killed if I ever told any one about the things that were happening. His exact words were "You and I will go fishing and you will not come back. I will kill you." The relationship then morphed into its sickest phase. I had to not only keep the secret, but I also had to work hard to make sure it remained a secret. I was certain that my life depended on it. I became a participant in the deception as it became overwhelmingly evident that there was going to be no rescue. I now knew that I would be spending the remainder of my childhood with Devlin--and he needed to be kept happy if I intended to survive.

Up to this point I had never been a witness to any of my siblings being sexually abused. I regularly witnessed them being beaten, jerked around by their hair, punched, kicked and called every damnable name that you could imagine. But I had no first hand knowledge of them being raped or molested, even though I was certain that they were. We only had to look into each other's eyes to know that. But then, if it were possible, life once again got worse.

Devlin then began to molest two children at one time. The horrible things that went on during those episodes are simply too difficult to repeat. Suffice it to say that we may never recover from those terrible images. While Devlin went on having his fun and while he remained arrogantly convinced that he would never get caught, I was having a nervous breakdown. Unfortunately, not even this caught anyone's attention. In those days people said stupid things like "Children are resilient. They bounce back." Well I am living proof that children are not nearly as resilient as some may think. Oh, I know that the experience didn't actually kill me, but we are now twenty six years removed from that hellish time and I have still not completely bounced back.

While others in my predicament may have felt the urge to consider suicide, I was beginning to lean heavily in the other direction. The extreme frustration of not being able to control any thing that was happening to me was turning into anger. My once innocent mind was suddenly fantasizing and dwelling on thoughts of revenge. As a boy growing up in Southern Mississippi, I was constantly exposed to firearms. I was given my first shotgun at age ten and was trusted to take it out hunting by myself almost immediately. That weapon was actually hanging on a makeshift rack, on the wall, directly over my bed. I also had a box of shotgun shells on my head board. I was too young to consider any legal ramifications, but I often laid there staring at that gun and fantasized about how easy it would be to make Devlin go away forever. When he would come home late at night he would have to traverse the long hallway toward his bed room, which made it necessary for him to walk right past the door of my bedroom. I shared a bedroom with my three brothers and I slept on one of the top bunks farthest away from the door. I could have very easily waited there in the darkness for him to pass by and blasted a slug through his chest. I was quite handy with that shotgun and seldom missed my target. I was not only considering this, but was literally trying to convince myself to go through with it. Often I fell asleep thinking just how close that gun was to me. I swear that it was the grace of God that kept me from committing murder. Considering what I was living through, it should come as little surprise to know that his wasn't the only murder that God saved me from.

In fact, he has actually intervened in similar circumstances no less than three times, sparing three separate lives, not to mention my own. I've already told you about my growing desire to end Devlin's life. Now allow me to tell you about the second person who God saved from an untimely death at my hands. We will have to skip ahead in the story for a minute, but bare with me.

I was thirteen years old and in the seventh grade. At the same time, there was another boy, who in this story shall be called "Tommy". Tommy was in my seventh grade class as well, but should have been a sophomore already. He had failed several grades and was a miserable train wreck of a human being. Now I don't know; He may have been suffering at home himself. I have no doubt that he was suffering at school due to his string of failures. But what ever his problem was, he had decided to turn his frustration outward and had become a genuine bully. This was a most unfortunate turn of events for me and my younger brother Nathan, because for reasons I'll never know, this bully turned his guns on us. He was several years older than us and a lot bigger. I suppose that given what we were enduring at our own home, we must have looked like easy targets to him. I'll just say that for the lion share of that year, he made our lives at school a living hell, and now we would have to be afraid at home and at school.

Eventually Nathan and I began to talk about this additional headache that we had inherited. The more we discussed it, the angrier we got. Eventually our anger reached a boiling point and just like that, we were no longer willing to tolerate being tormented at home and school both. Something had to be done, but what.

It may have been the years of pressure and fear that drew out such a level of anger in us, but for whatever reason, the death of this kid seemed to be the most logical solution to us. Again, we were just kids ourselves, and certainly not smart enough yet to think through what would have happened to us next. All we really knew was that we needed relief from this guy's constant attacks, and we were going to see to it.

We spent the next few days planning our retaliation and of course building up each other's courage for what was coming. Then the planning was done and it was time to kill. We genuinely were not afraid to do what we were about to do. Our conscience for this lad's well being had died months ago.

We figured that a rear ambush would have been the most logical plan of attack. One of us would exit the school bus directly in front of Tommy and distract him, while the other followed him and hit him in the head with a sixteen inch piece of number five steel rebar. We would then beat him to death.

As we rode to school that morning (with a steel rod concealed in Nathan's coat sleeve) we never uttered a word. In our minds, we were already picturing Tommy's death just outside the bus. We were not thinking of ourselves or, for that matter the extreme trauma that we were about to inflict on all of the children who were going to witness this violent murder. We certainly were not considering the pain that we were about to inflict on his family or ours. We were only thinking about killing the kid who would not stop tormenting us. As we pulled into the bus ramp at school, we looked at each other one last time, and then moved in for the kill. Tommy exited the bus first that morning, effectively eliminating our opportunity for the ambush. This was an unusual move for him, as he usually liked to linger. Oh well. No Problem. We will simply do it in front of his house after school.

A since of relief washed over me all day that day as I contemplated the end of this kid's rein of terror. Finally school would again be a quiet refuge from our other bully. About half way through the day, as I sat there in class staring at this kid, the miracle happened. He turned to me and made some snide remark about finding me after school. I just smiled. This poor kid was already dead; he just didn't know it yet. Just then, Tommy's dad walked into our class room with the principal. There was a quick inaudible discussion with the teacher and Tommy was told to gather his books. Tommy's father, having had quite enough of his constant failing and his lack of any real focus at school, decided to withdraw him completely and make him work in his produce store. I never saw Tommy again.

Nathan and I had no idea that God had just spared us both a possible life long prison sentence, while at the same time granting us freedom from our lesser nightmare. I know that Tommy had no idea what God had just spared him from and probably still doesn't. Nathan and I went home that day, threw away the pipe and returned to school the following day as if nothing unusual had occurred. What can I say? God is good. Let me just add that no one saw this coming. Tommy's death that day would have been the very last thing that anyone would have expected, and that was the real shame. No one saw what was happening to me at home and no one saw what was happening to me at school. I was invisible. No one would have linked any of that to Tommy's death for a very long time because no one was paying attention. That was 1978. We are thirty plus years removed from that near disaster and we've since had to learn the hard way that we most certainly should be paying attention to our kids at school. I really hope that we are now.

Well anyway, about that time I joined the Boy Scouts. They met only a few blocks from our home and it was another great avenue of escape from the house. Devlin seemed to encourage it and almost immediately I found that I really liked it. As a matter of fact I excelled at it. In no time at all I was a patrol leader and then a short time after that I was the senior patrol leader. It seemed that I was a natural leader. I earned every merit badge that I could get my hands on and was well on my way to becoming an eagle scout. What! Eagle Scout? Wait just a minute here! Weren't we just talking about a murder plot? Yes we were. And with the drama in my brain swinging from pole to pole like that, it was another miracle that I didn't end up going insane. But that was my life. I can tell you something else, now that I am a child abuse investigator, Devlin did not encourage my joining the Boy Scouts for no reason. My joining gave him access to a an army of possible victims.

Just prior to this colorful new scouting career coming to an end for me, I was granted the honor, while attending one of our spring camps, of being "tapped out" for the order of the arrow. I was immediately scheduled to attend the next order of the arrow initiation ordeal, which was one of the highest honors in the Boy Scouts. While waiting for the date of my initiation, my mother announced that she was again leaving Devlin. I'll talk more about that a little later.

I was twelve years old when I joined the Scouts and I thoroughly enjoyed that organization for several years before having to leave at age fourteen. The scout master of troop 4 in those days was a man by the name of Terry Demont. He was one of the only men that I actually felt safe with. In truth, there was no other man or woman on the face of the planet who had ever abused me in any way other than Devlin. But it was too late. I already had a profound phobia of being alone with any adult, especially men. Terry was a good man though. One who genuinely cared about these young boys and their future. He had to leave us due to a military career related move, but not before becoming one of the finest mentors any of us boys had ever known. He modeled true manhood for us, as well as good citizenship and he was missed. When he left us, he passed the baton to his assistant Mr. Charlie Dale. It takes an awful lot of sacrificed time and energy to properly lead a scout troop and Mr. Dale gave every bit the effort that his predecessor had given. He was another fine example for us boys to follow.

At precisely the time that I was joining the Boy Scouts, I was also discovering my romantic taste for the opposite sex. I didn't look much different than most average boys in my class--a bit scruffier around the edges, I guess--but it wasn't long before I discovered that a few girls actually liked me. Oh, man! Let me just say that having a cute girl tell you that she likes you has the most interesting way of lifting even the lowest of spirits. It's just that--well, let's face it--I was completely ignorant as to what girls my age needed, or what they even wanted for that matter. We've already discussed in some detail what I truly thought of females in those days and having never received any proper instruction or foundation in such delicate matters, these relationships were obviously doomed before they ever started. The dark realities of my home life were proving too heavy for even these rapturous moments.

It was also at age twelve that I took my first real paying job. It seemed that our local newspaper delivery lady needed some help folding all of those newspapers. She was offering one dollar and twenty-five cents per hour. But more importantly than the obvious huge financial opportunity, she was also offering a few more hours away from Devlin. It was my job to sit in her back seat and keep the folded newspapers coming, while she drove around throwing them out. It was also a perfect way to produce the five or six dollars needed for an evening at the skating rink. No kid in his right mind wanted to miss a Saturday night at the rink. Disco music and speed skates were just coming onto the scene and we had endless energy. We would have gladly kept on skating until the sun came up if they hadn't insisted on closing at midnight. So as anyone can plainly see, that job was extremely important to me; extremely important indeed. The dedication to my obvious work ethic was remarkable. Even I was impressed. Yes, sir, I was clearly on my way to the top.

I think I lasted a whole week before I quit. I don't know if it was the hours of country music or the ten years that she took off of my life with her chain smoking. I mean, don't get me wrong, she was a nice lady and all, but if I didn't want to die of lung cancer the following year, I had to get out of that back seat. So we parted ways and I was forced to find more creative ways to finance my social agenda. In fairness, I really didn't mind the country music. It was a different kind of country music in those days.

Devlin's family was a tight knit clan back then. They really are a great group of people. I have only fond memories of them. I suppose that he felt safe around them as well. He obviously felt that he could keep his second life safely hidden from them the way he kept it hidden from every one else. His mother and father, whom we affectionately called Granny and Papaw, lived in a beautiful, historic home on Lookout Mountain in Chattanooga, Tennessee. Having a mountain for a back yard made them extremely "cool" grandparents indeed. They accepted my mother and her three children as though we were their own and bestowed a tremendous amount of love on us. I still enjoy seeing them when I can. Devlin had five brothers and two sisters, who all treated us with the same affection that their parents did. They were all married and had kids of their own, which supplied us with a seemingly endless line of cousins to enjoy. These aunts and uncles really were good people and it is just a shame that I did not enjoy them more than I did. I was simply too afraid to be caught alone with them and so I ended up avoiding them most of the time. Now, to my knowledge, they had never hurt anyone in their lives and probably never would, but that didn't make me any less afraid. Allow me to give you a small for instance.

I remember one evening when I was around eight years old. Our family and several of Devlin's brothers and their families were all traveling across town for some kind of a family get-together. My brother Nathan and I were riding in the cab of a large flat-bed truck with two of Devlin's brothers. Something happened to the truck while we were still in rout, a flat tire or something. Anyway, this was the middle 1970s and there were no cell phones. We were also kind of in the middle of nowhere without even a pay phone. Even if there were one, there was no one to call because they were all in rout as well. So we simply waited for one of them to pass the same way, so that we could flag them down. How in the world did we ever survive without cell phones? I mean really. Well it was dark out and Nathan and I were all alone with these two men. Now they had only proven themselves to be kind and loving uncles who would have never hurt a soul, but my stomach was in knots. I kept thinking that their darker side would now reveal itself having been given this opportunity. Their idea was to get out of the truck and sit next to it while waiting for help. They sat near the front wheel and Nathan sat with them. I eased my way to the rear of the truck and sat behind it out of their sight. I wanted to call out to Nathan to join me, but feared that my warning might set them off. So I just sat quietly there in the dark. At that age, I should have been afraid of sitting alone in the dark, but my fear of being alone with adults far outweighed any childish fears of things that go bump in the night. I lived in a house with the worst monster of them all and had long since prioritized my fears. Dark places outside were in fact my companions in those days and not something that I was afraid of. Suddenly, I heard Nathan making a faint noise. My stomach sank as I immediately feared the worst. But then the sound was much clearer. He was laughing. As they all laughed, the two men beseeched me to join them. I politely declined their offer, fully expecting them to demand that I move forward. But they never did and Nathan never stopped laughing. They were only doing what any sane uncle would do given free time with a child. They were enjoying him and Nathan was obviously enjoying them. But I could not over come my fear. I know that they must have been wondering what was wrong with me, but I never left my dark quiet sanctuary until other family arrived to help us. That was a typical response for me when given similar circumstances. I now think of these uncles often and enjoy seeing them when I can.

Back to our story. I was twelve years old now and had already lived in four states and in at least six different locations. But I had already become wise in the ways of avoiding home time. Boy scouts, school, church, baseball and friends all offered many opportunities for me to steal away and find rest from the violent norm. All of this moving effectively prevented me from acquiring any lasting friendships and only added frustration to my already suffering education. While the abuse continued to go unchecked for the next few years, the beatings became progressively worse.

Let's talk about those beatings for a moment. If you happened to have the misfortune of being in line for a beating, you were in for a world of hurt and were literally overcome with dread. These often occurred to several children at once and the horror of being witness to another beating simply added terrible psychological ramifications. First the child was ordered to remove their pants and underwear, which resulted in instant humiliation and fear of the enhanced vulnerability to the belt. The child was then ordered to lie across the bed and not move. We were told that if we moved, rolled over, or got up we would just be beaten more. Devlin stood directly over the child and held only the belt buckle in his hand. The rest of the belt was hanging straight down, like some god awful whip. Then, with the swing and the intensity of a man who was trying to crush something that he hated, the blows would begin to rain down. I mean no exaggeration when I say that the man pulled back as to gain every bit of momentum that he could. He looked like a baseball pitcher winding up for a fast ball. When that belt would crash down onto the back, or butt, or legs of that child, it came with several excruciating effects. The initial blast was instantaneous pain. But before the child could even scream, the very tip of the belt, which was now being drawn back, would wrap around the child's body and snap like a whip, resulting in a hellish secondary blow. Actually, I remember that whip-like second blow hurting much worse than the first. The snap of those blows sounded terrifying to those who stood naked awaiting the same. Then there came the screams of the child who was being beaten. Very often and mostly out of sheer panic, the victim would roll away from the blow in an attempt to escape that secondary hit. This would infuriate Devlin, who was, in some sick way, counting on that second hit. He then promised many more blows until the child remained still. This was, of course, an impossible demand and the beating would usually only end after the child nearly passed out. Then, with that awful angry glare, he looked at his next victim and it started all over again. The bruises and the abrasions that were left in the wake of such violence often took as long as ten days to two weeks to heal. Even in the summer time, long pants and tucked in shirts were the norm. The number of such beatings through out the years were simply too many to be counted. They were Devlin's idea of corporal punishment and were liberally administered for such heinous crimes as disobedience or telling a lie. But mostly, they were handed out if Devlin simply believed that you disobeyed or lied. The children who lived in our home under his heavy tyrannical hand seldom disobeyed. If they ever found the courage to tell a lie, it was only being told in an attempt to avoid a beating for some other nonsense. There was never any convincing him otherwise. If it was in his mind to beat a kid, it was simply going to happen bar divine intervention. Thank God for divine intervention. Those miracles did occur from time to time, which certainly reduced the violence throughout the years.

Now there were, in addition to lies and disobedience, a number of lesser crimes which resulted in a variety of other mindless outbursts as well. For instance, if Devlin decided to waste a beautiful afternoon working on one of his old broken down jalopies and if, while being forced to assist him in the repair, you accidentally handed him the wrong wrench, you were immediately advised of the error with several blows to the head with that wrong wrench. Ping! Ping! Ping! Cue the stars. Those lumps also took many days to disappear. This was Devlin's way of teaching the child that they needed to be more mindful and pay closer attention to the task at hand. But once again, the true underlying reason for such behavior was that Devlin's ridiculous "control freak" brand of impatience always resulted in an outburst of rage which was always physically violent. Another of his favorite tools in his twisted ideology was to grab a kid by the hair of their head and violently jerk their head back and forth until finally throwing them to the ground. If this failed to relieve his frustration the child was then kicked, often more than once. It's a heck of a thing to see a child sail several feet across the floor after being punted like a football. In a side note, it should be remembered, that such violence was not reserved for the children only. More than a few times our mother was also on the receiving end of such reprehensible behavior.

The saddest part is that there was simply no end to these stories. I could do this all day long. I recall once doing something incorrectly while outside working with Devlin. Never mind what it was-- perhaps a wrong wrench or something. Anyway, I turned to make the correction and was unexpectedly hit on my back with the business end of a claw hammer. Bam! Unbelievable! There was simply no limit to this guy's cruelty. It connected on the muscle directly between my shoulder and my rib cage. My right arm immediately fell limp at my side and remained there because I couldn't move it. The seriousness of that blow had not yet fully occurred to me, as I was totally preoccupied with bracing for what I believed would be further blows. When they never came, I slowly transitioned to the shock of a paralyzed arm. I stared at my fingers for a moment and wondered why they were not responding to my will. There was no pain, just numbness from my shoulder to my finger tips. What on earth was happening? I thought, my arm worked a minute ago and now it was just as dead as an empty shirt sleeve. I don't really have the words to describe the fear that began to grip me. My skinny little arm remained useless to me for several minutes before finally coming out of its comma. Whew! That was close. Now I don't really know why, but I always believed that I would see some sort of remorse or perhaps a hint of sorrow on Devlin's face for the damage that he would cause, but I was always wrong. This fellow would simply return to his work as though he had done nothing unusual, leaving the kid to lick his own wounds. I could fill pages with such stories, but the arduous season of abuse would not last much longer.

Wasting away while faith grows

A most interesting and surprising irony to this story was also occurring throughout those torturous years; one which may lend explanation to my taking of a higher road later in life. It is also the only clear explanation that I can offer for the true healing that I now enjoy. While the years of sexual and physical abuse were tearing down my body and while the death threats and verbal abuse were ripping apart my mind--my soul, which by all accounts should have been cursing the day of its birth, was quite conversely being refreshed each day by a very powerful presence. I'm afraid that not even a gifted poet could adequately pen what I was truly feeling in regards to this presence, but suffice it to say that I never doubted who it was or why he was there. This is a little difficult to explain and although I say it at certain risk of sounding quite controversial to some of you, I do so with deep conviction, in the hope that you will at least hear me. I know very well how the mere mention of this subject usually exposes that ancient contrast, or should I say that invisible boundary, which seems to have always existed between some of us. And although I absolutely do not wish to alienate or in any way sow divisiveness here, I have always been acutely aware of that division. I also know, as I think we all do, that this message of a loving God and his grace has long sown that division by virtue of its own exclusivity; and has done so for thousands of years now. In other words, there will always be some who don't really care for the idea that God truly is the one and only Almighty creator and that he alone is absolutely sovereign and completely in charge of his entire universe. I think that they may also abhor the idea that he has provided for us only one way back to himself and that he has alone chosen that way without seeking any wisdom or input from his creation on the matter. The idea that God is God and man is not has sharply divided many millions of us for millennia and will likely continue to do so until the end of the age. That division notwithstanding, I suffer a powerful compulsion to speak to those who would hear me. I don't know any clearer way of saying it except to say that it is literally the most significant portion of my story, and is the reason for my survival and my eventual healing. I also feel a kind of an abiding indebtedness toward others who have suffered as I have and I fear I would certainly be doing them a great injustice if I were to yield to the common social pressures which often calls for me to hold my peace on the matter. In fact, it provokes me--even drives me--to love them and to not stop showing them the great relief that is now mine and the love that has so graciously led me from my dark past into this sweet freedom. It was without a doubt this miraculous gospel and its *refreshing* gift of grace that had alone bourn me to this long desired place of healing; an end which could never have been accomplished of my own will. And now, if you will allow me, I will show it to you.

I have, in fact, believed in God for most of my life. But can I just add and I say this rather tongue-in-cheek, a hardy "so what?" What I mean here is that anyone can say that they believe in God. Indeed multitudes have said just that, attempting to front their better nature. But unfortunately, merely *"believing in God"* has never really saved anyone. Believe it or not, our mere intellectual awareness of the Holy One has never been enough to complete God's equation for real salvation. In fact, the devil himself believes in God and hates him. Can we say that our own finite ability to believe in God is mightier than that of these fallen immortals who have actually seen him face to face? It's a good question and the answer is rather obvious. The truth is that salvation has never been found by those who simply believe that there is "a god" out there somewhere, but have never really known him personally or who have believed little else about him. Additionally, true justification has never been found by those who have taken that "god out there somewhere" concept and built an image of that god in their own minds, thus creating God in their own image instead of the other way around. This is, of course, just another example of man attempting to usurp control in order to minister to his own insecurities. I told you that this part might sound a bit hard, but with that said allow me to pose what I believe to be the most obvious question in regards to all of this. Considering that all matter and energy which exists in our known universe came into being long before the existence of man and quite without his pious intervention. And considering that man himself has always traveled through his short fragile life having never been able to conquer his own impotence in preventing the certain and inevitable end to his own mortal existence. Why then does he continually imagine that he will be able to do anything in his own power to save himself afterwards? Why does he think that he is even in a position to make any kind of sincere educated commentary on his future existence? Why indeed?

Another frightening misconception born in the mind of "man almighty" is the act of toiling his way to redemption. Let me just say here, since I've had some experience with this, that the act of filling one's life with religious duties will also produce absolute failure when attempting to procure that seemingly elusive favor of God. No matter how hard we endeavor to work to "deserve" righteousness, or attempt to earn the gift of eternal life, we always fall short. The fruits of our religious toil may yield for us a life far better than those around us, but it will never be able to produce a life worthy of heaven, at least apart from the King of heaven. It's like asking a man to swim a thousand miles for his own salvation. He may be a better person and a better swimmer than everyone else on the planet, but he'll never make it to shore unless someone saves him. Its just too far. At the end of the day, the whole question of how good he is or of how fantastic a swimmer he may be is deemed irrelevant. The relevant question becomes "Does anyone have a boat?" Don't take my word for it. Just ask the king of toil himself. No one in recorded history has ever striven to be as *duty* minded toward God in his attempt to deserve or to earn salvation than the great Apostle Paul himself. Not to sound pious here, but just for the sake of anyone who may not know who Paul was, allow me to give a little more detail.

Paul was not always an Apostle of the Lord Jesus Christ. He was once Saul, an absolute hater of all things Jesus. He was an extremely pious Jew and a Pharisee of the highest order. He was a leader of the Jewish religion and he abhorred this new Christian Church that was popping up everywhere. In his mind, the Jewish law reigned supreme and the thought of some unsanctioned messiah coming in and changing things terrified him, as it did most religious Jews. In his mind, the crucifixion of Jesus was just and should have brought a solid end to his strange message, but it didn't. He was now seeing Jesus everywhere in this new "sect" that they dubbed "Christians".

Saul's fury only intensified and his zeal to kill this movement seemed to double down. He then began a serious campaign (with the nod of the Jewish high council) of rounding up every Christian he could find and tossing them into prison. He also stood by and consented to the murder of an important Christian named Stephen. This man was serious about his hatred for Christianity.

It was while he was on his way to the city of Damascus, carrying letters from the Jewish ruling council (The Sanhedrin) which authorized him to further imprison Christians, that he had his historic encounter with the risen Christ. I'll give it to you in his own words which were recorded during a speech that he gave.

Acts 22:3-11 *"I am a Jew, born in Tarsus of Cilicia, but was brought up in this city. Under Gamaliel I was thoroughly trained in the law of our fathers and was just as zealous for God as any of you are today. I persecuted the followers of this Way to their death, arresting both men and women and throwing them into prison, as also the high priest and the council can testify. I even obtained letters from them to their brothers in Damascus, and went there to bring these people as prisoners to Jerusalem to be punished.*

About noon as I came near Damascus, suddenly a bright light from heaven flashed around me. I fell to the ground and heard a voice say to me 'Saul! Saul! Why do you persecute me?'

Who are you Lord? I asked. 'I am Jesus of Nazareth, whom you are persecuting' he replied. My companions saw the light, but they did not understand the voice of him who was speaking to me.

What shall I do Lord? I asked. He said 'Get up and go into Damascus. There you will be told all that you have been assigned to do.' My companions led me by the hand into Damascus, because the brilliance of the light had blinded me."

After that, he was a new man. The Lord had even changed his name to Paul. Saul the persecutor of the Christians was now Paul a leader among the Christians. But before that, he was still Saul the persecutor. Fanatic in his obedience to the Jewish Law of Moses, he tirelessly worked out his own righteousness for years. Driven in his religious zeal to "do" for God, he would eventually even murder in his name, while truly believing that he was doing God a service. No one, I mean no one had ever worked so hard to earn God's favor. But one little encounter with the risen Jesus and all of that instantly vaporized. A little later in his life, after having finally cast the entire weight of his meager faith onto the Son of God for salvation, he would gladly recount that all of his aforementioned pious duties, positions and accomplishments for God were, *"as dung and a total loss compared to the greatness of simply knowing his Lord Jesus Christ."* Wow!

So, if believing in God won't save us and if working for God won't save us, what ever will? The answer, my friend, quite possibly lies in just one single word of Paul's previously mentioned exclamation--"***knowing.***" The real question is again the most obvious. Do we really want to know him or would we really rather not? I mean, really, it's just about that simple, isn't it? We all eventually stand at that same gate of decision and wrestle with the worst part of our own selfish nature as we decide whether to step through. Because deep down, we all realize that if we choose to give in and **know** God, then, well we're now kind of stuck knowing him, aren't we. Once we know him, it becomes quite impossible to unknown him, doesn't it. In other words, the seat of authority can no longer be contested and those crooked lines of right and wrong become straight and well defined. But perhaps even more costly to our ego than any of this is the fact that we instantly know beyond any doubt as to whom we will give an account, both in this life and the one that is to come. This has been man's deepest struggle since the beginning of man. For in knowing God, man finally faces the devastating realization that he himself is not God. Countless souls throughout the ages have simply ignored his call and have walked past that narrow gate, opting rather for the much wider gate a little farther down the road. Satan has stood at the skinny gate for millennia, beginning in Eden itself, whispering his most effective lie to the masses that pass that way. "Why should God be God and not you? And why should you have to answer to him?" Be careful, my friends. He is cunning and he has no love for you. The answer to his riddle calls for humility, wisdom and a sober assessment of who we are in the universe. What else could explain man's excruciating difficulty with this whole creator/creation relationship? What else could keep all of us so divided and tripping over each other's theology? I am convinced that man's most significant struggles with himself and with others of his own species begins with his decision at that narrow gate and to which voice he chooses to follow. Will he listen to the one calling to him from inside saying "Come to me all you who are weary and burdened and I will give you rest for your souls?" Or will he believe the voice of the one who stands outside telling him that there is nothing even wrong with his soul and that he himself deserves to be the god of his own life. You mustn't yield to the latter. That one has hated us and lied to us from the beginning. We need only acknowledge that we have heard those two voices for ourselves and that we recognize the raging conflict in our own hearts for evidence of our long fall from grace. This great cosmic struggle is itself the proof that Satan is lying to us. In other words, we humans have indeed spiritually shipwrecked ourselves a thousand miles from shore, despite that devil's blustery speeches to the contrary. We're all treading water here and no matter how good you may think you are in comparison to those bobbing around you, you're never going to make it without a rescue. God save us from our own pride.

Anyway, that was it. That was the rich, unmerited favor that had been poured out on me during all of those dark years and eventually brought me to the place that I am today. When the boat came, I didn't resist. I fell into the hands of the rescuer and was saved. God had clearly revealed himself and his great love to me and at the age of nine I could not help but respond to it. This just means that I decided to transition from merely believing in God to actually knowing God. I couldn't shake the overwhelming sense that I was his child and from that time forward, our relationship grew. I know how that sounds to some, so I'll tell you what that doesn't mean. It did not mean that I suddenly turned off my brain, became an idiot and started acting like some sort of religious weirdo. I'll grant you that there is no shortage of those but that's not authentic and that certainly wasn't me. Nor did I suddenly start running around babbling about how spiritual I was or trying to impress my friends by regurgitating the latest metaphysical mumbo jumbo that I had seen on television the night before. As a matter of fact, no one ever really heard much at all about my faith in those early days, which is something that I now kind of regret. I mean, thinking back on it, I really should have been telling my friends and classmates about this awesome love and inner peace that had been given to me. It was just so pure and so real. But as unpretentious as it was, I had already become far too introverted for such evangelistic endeavors. God loved me anyway. He was actually pursuing me far more than I was him. That's just his way. Sometimes, I would ignore him for days, but so great was his affection for me that he happily maintained the relationship for both of us.

He's been passionately pursuing us that way forever. He really has. And I must say that this pursuit of his has brought me directly into his awesome presence on more than one occasion. Several times during my youth and always without prior warning, he would quietly come to me and visit with me. Yes! Just like that. I know how that sounds and clearly a little explanation is appropriate here. I'll do you one better than that. Allow me to invite you to have a look inside one of these private and very personal encounters.

It was the middle of the winter of 1978 in Columbus, Mississippi and I was twelve years old. It was late afternoon and I was already home from school and performing some of my everyday menial household chores. I was not even thinking about God. On the contrary, I was watching the clock in dreadful expectation of Devlin's soon arrival. I was vacuuming a floor as fast as I could so that I could hurry up and get finished and get myself out of sight by the time he got home. It was right then, in the middle of vacuuming that floor, that God surprised me with just such a visit. It was as sudden and as unexpected as getting hit by lightning. In less time than it would take the average person to blink their eyes, the room I was in was flooded with his overpowering presence. I literally felt him all around me. It's the most exciting and most terrifying feeling a human could ever have. My spirit was jumping up and down like a five-year-old on a new bed. My body trembled in fear as it became increasingly aware of its own weakness and fragility. The part of me that was jumping up and down wanted him to show himself, so that I could leap straight into his arms. The flesh and blood part of me felt like hiding its eyes and crawling under the couch. Suddenly all of that fear would evaporate as I would hear him whisper to my soul "Hi, Jimmy. I love you son. I'm always here with you. I'll never leave you alone." This was no emotional fantasy or escapism. My friend, when the God of all angelic host wants to visit a person--even a little person--he simply does it. The tears would run down my face as I attempted to respond to him, but I could never really get anything out. I was completely overwhelmed. Total peace like I had never experienced before flooded my whole body and I felt as though I were already in heaven. He would stay there with me in that capacity for a couple of minutes before finally replacing that all familiar vale which would render him invisible to my natural senses once again. And then, for the remainder of the evening, I feared no man--not even Devlin.

These memorable encounters occurred several times throughout those next few years and remain fresh in my mind to this very day. No burning bushes or fire in the sky; just him and his obvious love for me. And that's the way it was in those days. I just kept responding to his never ending love and he kept refreshing my spirit every day. That was it. That was the big secret. That's what was going on inside of me during those miserable days when everything else was going so wrong.

It's difficult to explain how something so terrible could be happening to a child on the outside while such a powerful faith in God was burning on the inside. But there it was. What I later came to realize was that suffering on various levels is a rather natural part of our journey here on the earth. Even though Devlin most definitely deserved to spend the rest of his life in prison for the countless unspeakable crimes that he had committed, we were not the only children suffering in the world and I knew it. At the very moment that I was suffering such hell at home, there were literally millions of other children all around the world who were themselves suffering god-awful things at the hands of powerful, uncaring god-awful men and women: famine, starvation, war, murder, slavery and every other kind of horrible exploitation that fallen man can perpetuate. I knew that what was happening to me wasn't the worst thing that had ever happened to a child in the world. It was just a very bad thing that was happening to me. I knew even at that tender young age that true life would not be found while I journeyed through the earth, but would come later, after this life. I also knew that no one would escape ultimate justice, because God, the righteous Judge, was seeing all of it.

I have often scratched my head and wondered how it is that we can rush so quickly to anger and blame God for all of the evil things the other humans were actually doing. We can spend an entire lifetime throwing around lofty phrases like "Where's the justice. God?" or "that's not fair God." One of the funniest observations that I have ever made in my life is how everyone seemed to be demanding and screaming for justice until justice was coming at them. Once they found themselves in its righteous cross hairs, they quickly lose their appetite for justice and would rather see mercy. What a fickle people we are sometimes. Do we really know what is *just* and what isn't, or what is *fair* and what is *unfair*? And why do the rules suddenly change when they no longer suit us? Even at the age of twelve, I knew that it was not fair that God's Son had to suffer and die for my sins. I knew that it would have rather been fair for him to remain at his Father's side while I suffered for my own sins. But he didn't. he who was entirely without sin came into this world that he had made and died for sinners. In doing so, he removed their sins and reconciling them to God. God was no longer holding sin against them. After he died for them, he did not remain dead. As it was explained in the Gospels and witnessed by hundreds of people, he rose again on the third day and returned to his Father to secure our justification. We were forgiven and now any one who wanted eternal life with God could have it for free. There was no need to earn it because we couldn't. And there was no way that we deserved it. But eternal life for us, which had just cost God everything, was now being offered as a free gift of grace through faith in Jesus Christ because of his great sacrifice. This is the very foundation of my faith which I had received as a young boy and which I have continually built upon to this day. It is that faith in such a great God and the knowledge of that wonderful place which I will arrive at after this life that has made me, despite all that I have been through, one of the happiest people in the world.

Dreams of Escape

This was my life for the next few years. The abuse continued and I distracted myself from it as much as I could. It was at this time that my mind seemed to turn earnestly toward various possibilities of escape. I was fourteen years old now and could run like a gazelle. I had been a Boy Scout for years and would have had no problem surviving in the woods by myself. I had guns, knives and access to plenty of outdoor gear. I knew how to fish, hunt and build shelter and fire for myself. I was convinced that I could remain in the woods undetected forever. In my youth, I failed to remember that I would only need to stay hidden for a few years until I became an adult. But day after day my mind would slip off into fantasy as I contemplated every detail of such an escape. I knew that no one could ever know of such a plan. I considered the eight or nine hour head start that I would have by simply stashing my gear in the woods near by, the night before. Then when every one else went to school and Devlin went to work, I would make my move. By the time every one got home and realized what had happened, I would be long gone. Remember that this was the 1970s and no school was phoning parents to inquire about absent children in those days, at least not any school that I had ever gone to. I also knew that once they realized that I had run away, they would tirelessly search for me. But with some stealth, camouflage and determination, I could easily evade such an effort. Never get comfortable. Keep moving from one location to another. Stay dry and warm. Never build a fire during the day since the smoke could be detected. If I needed to shoot some food, I knew that it would be okay. The sound of a shotgun blast in Mississippi was a common occurrence in those days and would draw no suspicion. The thought of being lost in the Mississippi wilderness did not frighten me in the least. Lost is what I wanted to be. I even considered the fact that I would be extremely vulnerable to sickness and injury, but simply filed it away in my mind as a calculated risk. I had won awards in leadership, survival skills and marksmanship. I was good at first aid and genuinely believed that I had a good chance to make it out there on my own. In ten years no one had ever attempted to rescue me and I had no reason to believe that any one ever would. The choice was becoming clearer with each passing day. Stay in this torment or save myself. I have to say now that I am older and can look back, I would have given myself an 85% chance of actually escaping and remaining undetected. But my true chances of survival would have quickly become negligible.

I don't know if it was a fear of hurting my mother with such a stunt, or God once again intervening and saving me from my own devices the same way he had saved me from committing murder so many times before. But for some reason I found it difficult to actually commit and leave. And then it happened again. My mom announced that she was again leaving Devlin and that Eli, Sarah, Carson and I would be going with her. It seemed I was to be spared the life of Grizzly Adams. Thank God.

CHAPTER SIX

A FAMILY REUNION

ONCE AGAIN I HAD NO idea as to the reason for our departure, but within a few days we had packed my mother's very large gold colored Cadillac with most of our belongings and hit the road. It was only recently that I discovered that she had actually all but caught Devlin in the act of molesting Eli and decided to leave him. And leave him we did. The soothing clickity clack cadence of the pavement dividers as the road went by seemed to mark the ever-increasing distance between me and my past. I was sure that it was for good this time. Grandma Kincer knew that we were coming and was once again preparing for our arrival. I was certain that we would be greeted with a baked ham, potato salad and corn bread sticks, along with her famous iced tea. Columbus, Mississippi to Florence, Kentucky is about a twelve hour drive under normal circumstances, but these were not. My mother was a relatively inexperienced long distance driver and her cross country navigation skills were also questionable. I was still only fourteen and barely knew my way to the next county. I had never driven any real distance, either. So I stayed in the seat next to her and together we did our best. Late in the journey, somewhere in southern Kentucky, we encountered an enormous amount of new road construction with all of its frequent lane changes and orange barricades. At fifty-five miles per hour an inexperienced driver can easily miss their exit and get lost in all of that. Our stress had just begun to peak when a torrential rain set in. It was now late evening and darkness was upon us also. The other three kids were fast asleep in the back, but mom and I were anxiously weaving our way through this maze of construction traps while that hard Kentucky rain just kept pounding us. Finally, our combined inexperience hit pay dirt. We thought that we had missed an important lane change that would have led us to an appropriate exit, but in fact we had not. If we had only continued a little farther down the highway, it would have become obvious. But instead, in one desperate moment of the blind leading the blind, I suggested to my mother that we should probably drive between the orange barricades and get into what we thought was the correct lane. In a second moment of utter brilliance, my mother heeded the advice of her fourteen-year-old son and changed lanes. In our minds, we were now resting easy in the knowledge that we had made it back onto the correct path. What we had in fact done was enter a closed construction lane. We had abandoned the speed limit hours ago and were crawling down the highway at a roaring twenty miles per hour. This was not a problem since we were, of course, the only vehicle in that lane. In a side note, this snail's pace was very likely the thing that saved our lives. Because just then, out of the dark rainy blur, there appeared a solid concrete divider wall which stretched all the way across our lane. We both screamed like little girls, but that only succeeded in waking up the other kids. A quick smash of the brake peddle and our doom was sealed. In one of the most surreal moments of my life, I watched and listened as that large automobile slid helplessly toward that wall and crashed into it with the most horrific sound I had ever heard. We had actually only bent the front right fender and punctured the battery, but in our panic we thought that the car was totaled and would soon burst into flames as we had witnessed so many times on television. That cold rain was still coming down pretty hard and even with the (imagined) imminent fire ball in our near future, we decided that it would be best not to get out and catch a cold. Brilliant! We just sat there for a few minutes and calmed down as we slowly began to realize that there would be no explosion. C.B. radios were all the rage back then and we certainly had one in the car, as did every other person on the planet in 1979. I had heard somewhere that the police monitor channel nine. I still don't know if that was actually true, but I tuned to that channel and called out like a professional "breaker 0-9, breaker 0-9 for an emergency." To my utter relief and surprise, a voice immediately responded, "Go ahead, emergence." In my usual tactful manner, I blurted out, "We need help. My mom just crashed the car and she's alone with her four small children." Other than Sarah bumping her leg, there were no real injuries to speak of and every one was fine. That nice man on the radio summoned help immediately and in no time a local ambulance arrived and took us all to the hospital to be checked out. The car was towed to a holding lot and my cousin Valerie drove down that morning to pick us up and drive us the rest of the way to Florence. The car was then towed to Grandma's house later that day. It was a miracle, but we were home again.

The reunions were as magnificent as they had been almost five years prior. Still, no one really knew what had been happening to us children. If they had known, they would have certainly come down on Devlin's head with a vengeance that he could not have imagined. But they did not know and were all just happy to see us again. By this time, a second prison was beginning to form around me. This one was the cold and lonely dungeon of shame and it was every bit as formidable as the first prison of fear. I did not know it then, but as I outgrew the prison of fear, this new one replaced it. It was even becoming too difficult to mention these appalling obscenities to God in prayer without feeling the urge to blush and turn away. The new prison would insure that Devlin's crimes would remain secret even though we were hundreds of miles apart. Even decades after any fears of mine had vaporized I was still incarcerated in that dungeon of shame, whose keeper was denial.

Any way, happier times were presently at hand and they were an easy distraction from the horrors which were now behind me. At least, that was my presumption. This was a most pristine environment. There were no dangers lurking around any corners in this place. I wasn't five years old any more or even ten. I was now fourteen and felt more light-hearted than ever before in my life. I sincerely viewed this as a turning point for us. I immediately began to absorb every reunion which came my way. Within a few short days my beloved Grandpa and Grandma Wischer learned of our arrival and again came calling. The following day, we were out at the farm, laughing and enjoying that sweet familiar country air. During our time out there, Grandma and Grandpa began to worry that mom would simply leave again. This concern was obviously not without precedence, so in a desperate attempt to prevent a loss of contact and to prevent us from simply slipping away again they decided to contact our dad, who was living in southwest Florida. Remember, we had not seen or heard from him for a decade. He and his wife, whom we will call Paula, immediately drove straight through for eighteen hours to reach the farm as quickly as they could. We had no idea that they were coming. I just remember being awakened in the middle of the night by Grandma and Grandpa and seeing my dad standing there next to my bed. We really didn't know what to say to each other. After an awkward hug and a few words of greeting we all went back to bed to continue the reunion in the morning. His arrival caught my mom completely off guard and genuinely frightened her. She could sense the increasing indifference that I was feeling toward her because of her constant determination to stay with Devlin through the years and she could also sense us beginning to slip away from her. We spent the next week or so reacquainting ourselves with our long-lost dad. He, along with Grandma and Grandpa, tried in vain to delve into our private hell. But we were totally convinced that not even they could help us and it was far too embarrassing to discuss anyway. **But they kept trying and, I must admit, nearly convinced us to open up.** When we simply would not, they left us with open invitations to talk to them any time we wanted to. This was to be the door for which I had been searching for years. Dad had to return to his business and his family in Florida, but not before leaving us with his phone numbers and address. We also gave him Devlin's address and phone number and knew that we would be staying in touch now. Man oh man; it seemed like nothing ever changed in Kentucky. It was great and it truly felt like home.

But something was different. Eli, Sarah and I were forever changed and it really began to show, especially in Eli and me. We had seen and learned a lifetime of violence and really knew no other way of life. The way we resolved normal sibling rivalries was through violence. Most arguments usually led to a physical fight. When these fights would occur in the presence of our brothers and sisters, they thought nothing of it. As far as we were concerned, this was the normal way to resolve issues. But this behavior left our family in Kentucky just baffled. We were no longer those quiet frightened boys who had left them five years prior. We were now very noisy, frightened boys. This physical violence between Eli and me would last until we were around eighteen years old. I think that on several occasions, we came dangerously close to unintentionally killing one another. But for now, we were home and that was all that mattered to us.

This trip was lasting much longer than the last one and with each passing day, it seemed to be more permanent. Mom actually had to apply for public assistance while she was looking for a job. This was a big step for her because she had spent the past decade as a "house wife" and had no idea what she was going to do to provide for us. We even discussed and dared to dream of getting our own apartment. This further solidified the separation from our past, but, unfortunately, it was not going to happen, at least not yet. For once again mom announced that she was retuning to Devlin. I suppose that she genuinely felt that she had no other choice. But this announcement at this particular time clearly unnerved me. As any mother could have seen, I was now actually reaching my breaking point. She didn't want to lose her boys and knew that if I was ever going to bolt, it would probably be now. This is the place where that prison of shame began to really sink its teeth into me. Since none of our family knew anything about any abuse, they all though that it was a good idea for mom to reconcile with Devlin. This would have been the opportune time to get the police involved, but the shame and embarrassment of mentioning these things to anyone was now far too much for me to overcome. Besides all of that, I had long since developed a fundamental belief that no one was really interested in helping me and that if I did call out for help, I would probably only succeed in procuring for myself more trouble than I already had. No, I was deeply convinced by then that no one was going to help me except me. Grandpa Wischer had spent a few days repairing mom's car, so once we were packed, we were on our way back to a truly unbearable existence.

Counting the Cost

During the drive back to hell, my frustration began to turn to anger. I had just suffered another heart-wrenching loss and was returning to be abused some more. Upon our arrival, Devlin could tell that rage was now brewing in me. He attempted to reassert his long-held authority with some stern words, but this only succeeded in making me angrier. I was still far too small to physically fight him, but it was now clear that he could no longer frighten my anger away. I had changed. I was becoming more and more independent in my thinking and my mother knew it. She also knew that I was bent on leaving and this also frightened her.

Eli and I began to talk frequently about telling our dad about what had been happening to us, but we could not seem to break through that vicious wall of shame. You have to remember also that we were not at all convinced that anyone, no matter how well intended, could actually help us. **Ten years of the entire world appearing totally impotent in the**

face of what had been devouring us had taught us to trust no one.
The conversation that Eli and I kept having was paramount to counting the cost. Was it really worth the humiliation or the possible repercussions to at long last chance a cry for help? What if no one believed us? What if they do believe us, but tell us that there is nothing that they can do for us? What if we tell everything and get murdered before anyone had the time to get to us? If we leave well enough alone, then at least we will live. These were all very real problems with which two young teenage boys had to regularly grapple. It was an extraordinary time of deep soul searching as each sought to gain some courage from the other. The excitement between us was building as though we were each trying to convince the other to jump out of an airplane for the first time. You go first. Oh no, you go and I will be right behind you. We knew that it was almost green light jump time and could just about see each other's heart beating through our shirts. Mom had seen us talking privately like this and I'm sure she suspected something, but absolutely no one knew what we were discussing. No one knew any of the other terrible questions that we had to sort out either. For instance, what if we pulled this off and escaped? What will happen to the rest of the children? It was very likely we would never see them again. We might also never see our mother again--at least not for a very long time. But worst of all, we knew that we could be on the eve of our own deaths. How could we tip the odds to be more in our favor? No matter how it played out, I was pretty sure that we were in for some extreme violence and would certainly need a contingency plan for hiding out until help arrived. We had hiding places that Devlin was aware of and others he had no idea about. Of course, all of these well-laid plans may prove useless once the crap actually hit the fan, but nevertheless these were the things that we were talking about. And suddenly the time was right.

It's now or never

It was a "normal" Wednesday evening for our "family" in the summer of 1981, when I had finally decided that the time was right. July meant that there was no school the following day and we would be awake a little later than usual. Devlin religiously attended a poker game on Wednesday nights and usually came home around two or three in the morning. It was around nine in the evening now and we decided that it was time to make our move. Our plan was to sneak into the dining room, which was near the very front of the house, while mom and the other children were watching television in the family room at the other end of the house. Once in the dining room we would use the phone which was mounted on the wall and call our dad down in Florida. Once the call was placed, we would walk into the formal living room and close the door. Remember that this was occurring in 1981. There was no cordless phone with which to sneak outside. This phone had a cord which severely limited our mobility. Once in the living room, we would tell our dad everything and hope that he would be able to help us. Dad immediately knew that something was wrong because of the hour in which he received our call. We told him that we were in trouble and needed help right now. He said "Ok you got it. What do you need? What's the problem?" Eli and I struggled through the embarrassment for nearly ten minutes before one of us and I think it was Eli, finally told him "We're being molested." There was a long silent pause as Dad tried to keep his emotions in check. Then, with a crack in his voice he said "God, I'm sorry, boys. I was afraid that something like that was happening to you." He asked for more detail, but we could not bring ourselves to divulge anything more. He then said "Okay, hang up right now and call the office of the Clerk of the Circuit Court. Their number is in your phone book. They will believe you and will send help to you right away. Once you've made that call, then call me right back and we'll take the next step." We did as he instructed and actually spoke to someone within the next few minutes. I do not remember the entire conversation, but I do remember telling them that we were being abused and needed help. The lady who we were talking to asked "Are you in danger right now?" What she actually meant was, now that it's hitting the fan, are you going to be in any danger or do you need intervention right now? We mistakenly took the question literally. Devlin was not due home for hours and as long as he was not there we felt relatively safe. So we told her no. She then told us that she would send the 1980s equivalent of a child protection case worker out to our house in the morning to help us. We thought that that was okay as long as no one else knew what was happening until then, so we agreed. As she was giving us some last minute instructions, we heard our mom approaching from the back of the house. We quickly exited the living room just in time to hear her demand "Who are you talking to at this hour?" We said "No one" and abruptly hung up on the nice lady. Mom then demanded "Don't lie to me! Who were you talking to?" We again said "No one. We were just messing around with the phone." The words barely left our lips and the phone began to ring. I quickly said "I'll get it!" But mom said "Oh, no you, won't!" She answered the phone and listened for a few seconds before blurting out "Who is this?" I knew then that we had just passed the point of no return. The fan was running and the crap was flying. Mom hung up on the lady again and demanded "What have you boys done?" I said "Mom, we're being abused by Devlin and we want to leave and live with our dad." My mother then began to panic and made one of the very worst decisions of her life. She called Devlin at his poker game and told him what had just occurred. She wasn't trying to keep us from escaping the abuse. She was just terrified that her family was exploding and that she was literally going to lose her boys that night. I also know that she called him out of fear of what he may do to her if she didn't call. What makes a woman stay in those circumstances? What is it that seems to so easily take away a mother's protective instinct? Is the money really that powerful? I mean she just kept running back to him. And now she was sicking him on me.

Anyway, this was the hard part. This was the part we dreaded most. She had clearly chosen him over us and we knew that he was now rushing home and once he arrived, we would be alone with him. I somehow always knew that it would come to this. There was not going to be any Clerk of Circuit Court in that room with us. There was not going to be any child protection case worker or police officer in there with us, either. Our dad was certainly not going to be in there with us. We were going to have to face him alone. I calculated that even at high speed, it was going to take him around twenty minutes to get home. So during that time, Eli and I just sat there contemplating our fate. You can not begin to imagine what was running through our heads at that moment. All those years of death threats were now literally coming toward us like a raging bull. We never said a word. We just sat there staring at each other. Our eyes were communicating volumes as though they were speaking out loud. Should we run for it? But what we had not counted on was the overwhelming sense of exhaustion that would finally hit us. And it did hit us at exactly that moment. The fear and the anticipation had utterly sapped us of any energy and, besides, we simply did not want to run away from this any longer.

We watched as Devlin drove recklessly into the driveway as though hell itself was chasing him. He entered the house in a rush, with a panicked look on his face. I took a deep breath and thought to myself "Here we go." Devlin looked at me and said "Let's go." He, mom and I walked into their bedroom and closed the door. I sat on a chair and he and mom sat facing me at the end of their bed. Mom was there, I'm sure, to act as some kind of mediator. Devlin said "What are you doing? What is it that you want?" An unusual sense of calm came over me at that moment and I looked directly into his eyes and said "We want to go live with our dad." We didn't have to tell him why, in fact "why" never came up in the conversation at all. He knew very well why. The next thing he said truly caught me by surprise. I was bracing myself for some real violence when he said "Why didn't you just say so? You could have gone any time you wanted to. You didn't have to call anyone." I didn't know how to answer that. He was a pathological liar and was certainly only thinking of himself at that moment. I knew this to be a fact and could only sit there and stare at him in disbelief. He then said "I'll buy you a ticket tomorrow if you want." I said "Me and Eli." He responded, "Yes. Just call these people back and tell them that you were just mad at us and it was a lie. If you will do that for me, I will buy you a ticket to Florida tomorrow." It sounded too good to be true. But he looked truly desperate. I could see it in his eyes. I was now faced with a bigger dilemma than I had bargained for. Could it actually be as simple as that? Or was I being played? You must remember that I truly trusted no one, including this so-called child protection case worker that was supposed to be coming in the morning. And having been given the choice to believe whether any adult would actually be able to help me, I chose to remain dubious. Either way, it was going to be a tremendous gamble for me. And I was gambling with Eli's life as well. Since I did not know the person who was coming in the morning, I decided to take my chances with Devlin's desperation. So I said "Okay." To which he responded with a deep sigh of relief, saying "Alright then. Let's make that call." His face then turned red with anger as I had gained the upper hand. With all of the deep-seeded hatred of a demon possessed individual, he said to me, "Jimmy, the only reason that I don't get my gun and kill you right now is because I promised your mom that I wouldn't." I felt like saying "Whatever. Just shut up and buy the tickets." But I remained silent. As far as I was concerned, we would never have to have another conversation as long as we lived.

I went back into the kitchen and called that nice lady again. I kept my end of the bargain and told them that it was all a lie. She then told me that they would have to come out in the morning anyway and **see** for themselves. No amount of apologizing could dissuade her. So I was now going to have to make one more performance before I could get those tickets. Devlin diligently coached and rehearsed with us the finer points of deception until he felt that we were ready. The following morning, he went to work and I waited the arrival of whomever it was that was coming. True to her word, she did come. We went into the den and sat on the couch. I am convinced even to this day that she thought that she was just responding to another waste of time, because the entire interview lasted less than five minutes. She said something like "Is anyone hurting you? Are you sure? You know it's not good to lie? You could get into a lot of trouble telling lies like that." And then it was over. I guess that was her version of **seeing** for herself. No inspection of the children to look for signs of physical or sexual abuse. No other interviews with the remaining five children in the house. She just left. I would like to say that I felt terrible afterwards. But the truth was I didn't feel much of anything anymore. I mean really, I was prepared to take Eli and abandon the other four siblings to their fate. I wasn't certain that I was going to be able to pull even that off. Those past ten years had literally robbed me of every ounce of the compassion that I had once possessed.

I had to call Dad later that day and tell him about the deal I had struck. He was as skeptical as I was, but agreed to wait and see. I now believe that he should have been screaming at me to call the lady back and get the police out there-- if what we had told him was true, then it is now time for this fellow to go to prison for the rest of his life. But we just waited. Devlin came home from work that evening and said "Thanks. I got your tickets, but your flight doesn't leave for a few days." Had I not seen the tickets with my own eyes, I would not have believed him. I am sure that he purchased a later flight in order to try to convince me to remain quiet about the abuse once I got to Florida. He would say things like, "They will put your mom in prison too, you know, not just me. Is that what you want? And your brothers and sisters will be put into a reform school since there will be no other place to put them." I cringed at the thought of my mother going to prison. That was something that I simply was not willing to gamble. My God, it was sounding more and more like I was the bad guy in all of this. I really was starting to believe that I was the one who caused all of this mess for everyone. It was just one more dysfunction that would have to be unpacked later in life. Nevertheless, a few days past and Eli and I found ourselves on a flight to Tampa, Florida.

CHAPTER SEVEN

FIRST PEACEFUL SLEEP

We landed in Tampa at around nine o'clock in the evening and were met at the gate by our dad, Paula and their four children whom we will call Melissa, Leeann, Trevor and Deborah. With cheers and hugs we were genuinely welcomed, despite what we must have looked like to them. I'm sure that Dad had somewhat prepared them for what they could expect. We were overwhelmed and really couldn't say much as we were swept from the gate and out to the parking lot. It was mid-July and no one could have prepared us for the 90 % humidity that we would be walking into. We literally found it difficult to breath. I remember our new siblings laughing as one of them informed us that it had just rained and that it was actually much cooler now than earlier in the evening. Once in the car, we sucked in the cooler climate and slowly came around. They filled our ears with conversation all the way to their little house out in the suburbs. We didn't mind though. We couldn't get a word in anyway so we just sat quietly and enjoyed all of this new attention. Upon entering their home, we noticed a large banner which the children had lovingly prepared for our arrival. If I remember correctly, it read "Welcome home Jimmy and Eli." We were far too stripped of our humanity to really appreciate the genuine love that was being extended to us. Thinking back on it, I hope that our general lack of emotion didn't hurt their feelings.

I didn't know it then, but Dad and Paula were making a tremendous sacrifice in adding two teenage boys to their already crowded home. They weren't rich. On the contrary, they worked hard every day to provide for the family they already had. Two more only made for tighter quarters and tighter purse strings.

Anyway, we sat up and talked for a little while and then went to bed. Eli and I were assigned to Trevor's room. He was around nine years old at the time and seemed happy to have the company in his room. He took the top bunk, Eli took the bottom and I slept on a fold-up rollaway bed. It was the most comfortable bed in the world that night, because for the first time in a very long time, I felt genuinely safe. There was no way that Devlin could get to me in that house and for the first time in years I drifted off to a peaceful sleep believing that no one in that house wanted to hurt me. It was the best sleep that I had ever had.

Our first few days were spent being assimilated into the every day function of that family. Emergency procedures were rehearsed in case Devlin tried to make an unannounced visit. Chores needed to be assigned along with new sibling boundaries and, at least for a little while, everything seemed to be routine. Other than the fact that it literally took months for Eli and me to get used to the tropical climate, everything looked as though it was coming together and that this new family arrangement might just work. But then reality hit.

Dad and Paula had, in fact, made a remarkable miscalculation in the undertaking of this new commitment. Although their hearts seemed to be in the right place, they were in point of fact completely ignorant as to whom and what they had just invited into their home. This was no ordinary case of two poor orphan boys in need of a family. These two boys had just come to them from a very dark place indeed; a place where for ten straight years they had been continually raped, molested, beaten, verbally smacked around and threatened. These two boys arrived with suitcases full of dysfunction and were actually in need of a considerable amount of mental health therapy. They weren't mentally retarded or handicapped. But psychologically, they had been torn to pieces. In reality, they should never have gone to live with that family, at least not at first. In retrospect, what really should have happened was that Devlin should have been charged with numerous capital felonies and hauled off to serve a life sentences. The children should have then been safely removed from that house and all six given the essential medical and psychological help which they so desperately needed. Of course, this never happened, so there we were in our new home in Florida and none of us equipped to handle what was coming next. The outcome was unfortunately inevitable as the many hidden troubles which had taken root in us years and years prior would soon begin revealing themselves to the astonishment and dismay of our new family.

I remember being some what taken back by the relatively sober conclusions that these kids could arrive at during their regular sibling rivalries. Although it was certainly I who was the brutish misfit, they seemed weak to me. They were literally able to solve their problems with a few words and not much else. When Eli and I found ourselves in the middle of any such dispute, whether it was with each other or anyone else in the family, the end was always precluded by a barrage of foul name calling and violent threats. This was a nifty little trick that we had picked up along the way from Devlin. If the language failed to achieve the desired end, it was then certain that physical violence would erupt. When I say physical violence, I mean just that. A garden variety melee would usually include punching, kicking, thrown elbows and an assortment of knee spikes to the soft tissue. We had learned from all of the blows that we received from Devlin over the years what really hurt and what didn't. So if you were in the chair that I had already called, and you wouldn't heed the warning to move, then you deserved a knee spike to the kidney. That was normal for us.

I really cannot speak for my four new siblings, but I can only imagine that our violence must have been quite a shock to them. Dad and Paula found themselves in the middle of a full-time refereeing job, while simultaneously trying to avert a complete implosion in their family. The sheer weight of their ignorance as to what they had gotten themselves into immediately began to take its toll on their marriage as well as each family member individually. Anyone who didn't know what had happened to us during the previous ten years would have been left to conclude that we were simply a couple of undisciplined monsters. In all actuality our inner demons and psychological deficiencies were the extent of our monstrosities. We had never touched any illicit drugs or drank any alcohol. We never cast our lots into any criminal enterprise or even spend time with those of the baser crowd. Externally, we were a couple of average kids, but emotionally we were a train wreck. There was just too much anger and frustration and fear trying to burst out of us. We were only making it worse by suppressing it or by forcing it all back down in an attempt to behave or fit in. The inner pressure would build to its volatile point until the inevitable would periodically occur and the geyser would once again blow, temporarily filling our immediate atmosphere with a bluster of steam and noise. These fairly predictable mini-eruptions were usually manageable. But peering through the façade of containment, one could easily see the eerie foretelling of a coming mega-eruption. These boys really needed help.

We simply had no idea how to process what we were feeling or how to effectively communicate it to those around us. Even a brief glance at our intellectual style of reason, when viewed through the lens of a more balanced world view, revealed that we were genuinely warped and contorted. Our decisions were mostly survival oriented and far less community minded. Consequently, our conclusions often left those around us scratching their heads in wonder. The way we related to our mother during this turbulent season was a classic case in point.

Our mom had stayed in contact with us by phone as much as she could. Hers was the familiar voice that always brought us to calm harbor during those past stormy years. We weren't angry at her even though some thought that we should be. She had never abused us and the truth was we loved our mother and probably would continue to do so no matter what. Anyway, I guess after a couple of months of missing her boys she decided that she wanted to bring us back. We told her that we loved her, but that she needed to be clear that we were entertaining absolutely no thoughts of ever returning to that hellish place. I hoped that would have been enough to cool her jets, but the longing to see us again had obviously become too much for her to bear. With maternal instincts now driving her emotions, it came as little surprise when she played her custody card in an ill advised attempt at forcing Dad to send us back to her. I remember telling her that she really needed to leave it alone. I reminded her that the deal was that Eli and I would live with our dad and that in return we would not tell on Devlin. She didn't want to hear any of that and told me that if we did not come back right away, she would ask the courts to force us back and that we would not see our dad any more. I became angry and told her that if she wanted to go to court, then to court we would go. She replied "You do whatever you think you need to do." So true to her word, she petitioned the courts to send us home. Dad stepped up and asked the court to hear our story and our reason for not wanting to return. The Judge agreed and we were instructed to talk to some court liaison councilor. Eli and I were taken into a rather large room, where we sat down with this polite fellow at a rather large table. As we began to reveal to him the brutal and demoralizing details of our childhood, he abruptly stopped us and hurried out of the room. I don't know why; maybe it was all just too terrible for him. What ever his reason, one thing was certain, that little five minute meeting was over; and that my friend was the last time that we were ever asked in court to talk about our ordeal. I was not privileged to witness the conversation that took place behind closed doors after that, but by day's end, our dad held legal custody of me and Eli. Mom was visibly crushed, but I must admit that it was a giant load off of my mind. I still don't know why the Judge, upon hearing the allegations, never demanded an investigation. I understand that it was just a custody hearing, but, my God, he was a judge. How does an officer of the court hear something of that magnitude and not investigate? I don't know why the councilor or even my dad never demanded one either, but once again the more significant part of the story was simply swept under some rug: out of sight and out of mind. I'm not sure how true this is, but Dad made it sound like the Judge used the sexual abuse allegations to quickly make this custody issue go away. He said that Devlin and our mother were told by the judge that they had better shut their mouths and relinquish custody or he would almost guarantee that they would both be going to prison. So they swallowed their pride and signed the papers. Then they simply allowed Devlin to walk out the front door. As he once again strolled past the gates of justice, the councilors gave us a wink, as though they had genuinely won some kind of acceptable consolation victory for us. Now I know that we have one of the finest criminal justice systems in the world, but this was an absolute disgrace. I really hate to say this, but I feel that I must. I am convinced that the issue of child sex crimes had not yet received enough hair-raising publicity in the 1970s and early 1980s--and still may not have. I think what I am trying to say is that, unfortunately, not enough children had been brutalized or butchered on television yet. I know that sounds horrible. But nothing seems to get the masses screaming and the politicians hopping in the right direction like extreme tragedy splashed across our television screens during the Six O'clock News. Now that's a tragedy in of itself, but it's one that keeps revisiting itself upon us every now and then. All this took place in 1981 and, although we have made some progress in the way we sentence convicted offenders, I fear that they still have somewhat of a slippery advantage at times. Now I'm not a total cynic on this subject. I concede that some of them do get adequately prosecuted and go to prison for many years, but others are still escaping with much lighter penalties, if they are punished at all. Oh, yeah I guess they also get their nifty new "sex offender" title. Wonderful! That should save the day. This is the part that troubles me. How much proof do we need before we finally admit the truth? We know very well how extremely dangerous these people are. We also know very well that many of them refuse to rehabilitate. They're not regular criminals! I repeat. They are not regular criminals. We have to wake up and start recognizing them for what they truly are. They are dangerous predators and they simply must be categorized and warehoused as such for the safety of society. You will not change these people. You can't make a lion stop wanting to eat gazelles and you will never make the child predator stop wanting to have sex with children. It's simply too late for them. I'm really not trying to just sound mean here. It's a fact--it really is too late for them. They have a genuine taste and a real appetite for deriving sexual gratification from children. The same way normal adults have tastes and appetites for regular consensual adult sexual gratification. I know how incredibly sick that sounds, but that's how it is with them. Asking them to "rehabilitate" means asking them to quit having their sexual tastes and appetites. Can you just stop having your regular adult oriented sexual appetites? Do you suppose that you can be rehabilitated to stop having them? No. So what are we trying to accomplish here? We also know very well that a percentage of these folks are going to *"re-offend"*, which is just a nice way of saying they are going to rape, molest or even kill another child. In the world of criminal offenders the statistical and behavioral information that we have gleaned from thousands of investigations present us with the gloomy prospect that child predators will always represent a very high risk. Although we don't know which ones, we do know that some of them are simply going to re-offend. It's not a question of *if;* it's really only a question of **when.** The awful evidence to what I am arguing here has come to us at a staggering price and the people who have had the misfortune of paying that price will never recover what they have lost, at least not in this life. For instance, did that *"sex offender"* title do anything to save poor Jessica Lunsford, who, in 2005, was kidnapped from her bedroom while she slept, brutally raped for days and buried alive by a convicted sex offender? I hate to state the obvious, but I think this proved the impotence of merely attaching a label to a child molester. Anyone who knows anything about this subject knew that John Cooey was at risk to re-offend. So what were we thinking? I mean really, that's a fair question. What in God's holy name were we thinking? Were we just going to turn him lose and hide our heads in the sand and hope for the best? And we could fill a book with examples like these.

Now if I may, by way of a brief side note, just say for the record what I feel and what I am certain that many of us privately believe, but never say out loud. I am not talking about these late teenage love affairs where one of the unfortunate lovers has discovered that they have exited the world of juvenile status and have technically become an adult. I get it that we have to draw that line somewhere and that they should certainly find themselves in some measure of trouble for showing such open contempt for that line. But should they be shackled to that same sex offender ball and chain for the rest of their lives as the real rapist? My God, half the universe would be titled sex offender if the truth were known. No, my thoughts in this book are exclusively aimed at those who truly victimize others, primarily anyone who preys on children. Well, that's just my opinion. Anyway, that said; let's get back to our story.

I've been in the law enforcement community long enough and have rubbed elbows with the judicial community long enough to have clearly seen some of the very complex problems that vex us in terms of effectively apprehending and prosecuting these offenders. The previously mentioned sex offender title, while on its surface sounds like an effective tool, is actually quite powerless in restraining a man or woman who is bent on re-offending. With statistics showing any kind of re-offence rate, this title is clearly not enough. As a matter of fact, with any percentage of re-offence, I would feel tempted to argue that we should offer absolutely no level of freedom for any convicted child sex offender. The problem with this line of reasoning lies in the judicial and constitutional roadblocks that we often encounter on our quest for a successful prosecution. For instance, the bad guy is always presumed innocent until proven guilty. Since the State bears the burden of proving this guilt beyond a reasonable doubt, they will often not even attempt to prosecute the case for fear they lack the evidence to prove it. Nothing stings the ears of an investigator like hearing the prosecutor say that they sincerely believe the child is being abused, but they can't prove it. I wasn't kidding when I said that these guys are hard to catch and get prosecuted. We don't call them predators for no reason. But what really hurts is catching them and having the evidence to successfully prosecute them, only to watch them make a deal with the State which will guarantee them a much lighter sentence and a parole date. This is where I believe that we need to rethink our methods. I understand that the state has a budget and that they wish to save the time and money by avoiding a trial if possible. I get this and I agree with it for the most part--except for when it comes to serial killers and sex offenders; especially child sex offenders. I also know that the State often wishes to spare the victim the additional trauma of having to testify in court against their attacker. I don't want to see them have to go through that either. But I believe that if the possibility exists for an effective prosecution of an offender, then it should be done aggressively, and that, if convicted, the sentence should always be life without the possibility of parole. This would afford us two immediate benefits. The first benefit would be our certain comfort in the knowledge that this offender would never again have the opportunity to prey on another child. The second would be the potent message sent to others of their kind.

Many states have made the prosecution of these people so ridiculously complex regarding victim ages and dates of occurrence that it's almost depressing. Then there are the children who are raped by these predators, but at an age where the crime is no longer considered a capital or life felony. Let me give you a true life example. A stepfather sexually molested his twelve-year-old stepdaughter over a period of time. But since the crimes were committed after her twelfth birthday, they were considered a lesser crime and were actually reduced to a lesser felony; which subsequently carry with them "statutes of limitation". This is not good, because now the victim had only a limited amount of time to reveal what happened to her. Once that time had passed, the perpetrator simply got away with his crime. Again, that was absolutely a true incident and every time I think about it, I get sick. All I can think is: are you kidding me? It often takes decades for victims to break out of their mind prisons and report the crimes that were committed against them. We desperately need to rethink some of these gigantic holes that exist in our current criminal code. They are only working to the advantage of the perpetrators and are allowing these hyenas' crimes to, at a minimum, go unpunished and at a maximum, simply go on. Now to me the answer to these riddles is almost over-simplistic. But if your answer to these same criminal justice perplexities should be as lame as a concern of prison overcrowding or money, then I should be left to conclude that you have not given this problem any real thought at all. In fact, you are literally saying that overcrowding and money shortages are a good enough reason to brush off the death of Jessica Lunsford and the countless rapes and murders of thousands of other children. If you are occupying a public office and you feel this way, your constituents should remove you from that public trust at their earliest possible opportunity. Your refusal to act on their behalf regarding these dangerous people speaks volumes to the ones who elected you and should no longer be ignored. For public officials there is no gray area or middle ground here. You are either an asset or a liability in this fight. You were elected to work for the citizens who gave you your job. That work is often hard and requires courage and sacrifice to benefit and protect those citizens. If this is not something that you are willing to do, then go home. My over-simplistic observation to all of this is that if John Cooey had been in prison where he belonged, Jessica's family would still have their baby girl and we all know it. I can also assure you that no amount of clever political whimpering can deflect or drown out this glaring indictment. It's sickening to see such a reverse in roles these days, but some of our judges and politicians have developed a bad habit of not listening to the people and have instead become comfortable politely telling their constituents to stay out of the grown-up discussions while implementing their own clever policies such as making deals with and releasing sex offenders. I don't know whose idea that was, but I'll guarantee you that if you ask the American people what they think about the issue, you would have a very different answer indeed. I've been alive long enough to know that few things disturb the American people more than a lazy whimpering politician who refuse to bend to the people's will and renegade judges who would rather play legislator from the bench than do their job and protect the community who elected them to that bench.

I apologize if this last bit sounded like the rantings of a bitter man. But in keeping with the truest spirit of this book, I feel that I must record everything just as it actually happened, including what I was feeling at the time and my thoughts after the fact. Now although I was only fifteen years old in the courthouse that day and could not yet articulate my strong feelings on this matter as I just did, you can be assured that they were indeed troubling me even then. Of course, having received no psychological help up to that point, one could clearly see how this frustration was beginning to work itself out in a very unhealthy way.

That first summer was soon over and a new school year had arrived. Maybe this would bring the much needed relief to our embattled family after spending those first few months crammed into that little house together. The courts had also facilitated a few sessions for the entire family with a real psychologist. I think that we went four or five times, but it just became too difficult for Dad to drive us all the way across town every week, so we just quit going. This was a huge mistake. This was exactly what Eli and I needed, but once again it would have to wait.

About that time and as if things couldn't get worse for me, we received word that Grandpa Wischer, who had been fighting lung cancer for some time, was finally losing that battle. I had not been able to see him or visit with him for a couple of years and upon hearing this horrible news, I wanted so desperately to just be there with him. I felt that I was about to lose him again and the thought of not being able to tell him to his face that I loved him and that I would miss him was just killing me. Given their financial situation, Dad and Paula had no intentions of going up to be with him, so I was stuck. These are most definitely the times when it totally sucks to be a penniless, powerless teenager. Of all the people in the world that I should have been able to say goodbye to as they depart this life and enter the next, he was certainly at the top of the list. This was just terrible. My heart was only lifted again upon hearing the fantastic news, that during his illness, he finally relented from a life of cynical atheism and had thrown his trust onto the Son of God. Although his passing was a tremendous blow to me, I took great comfort in the knowledge that I would certainly see him again. It just seemed so unfair that the man who truly loved me the most in this life would have to be deprived of my company for so long and die a thousand miles away from me. I look forward to a reunion from which there will be no more sorrowful departures.

About that same time, Devlin and mom moved from Columbus Mississippi to Sarasota, Florida, roughly fifty miles south of where I was living in Tampa. The courts had temporarily removed Nathan, Rebecca, Sarah and Carson from Devlin's house, but eventually allowed them to return. This is something that I will explain a little later. We were still not angry at our mother and were eager for her to drive up to Tampa with the other children and visit us. I will never be able to describe the feeling of actually seeing them after so many months. My reunion with my baby brother Carson was particularly sweet. The visits were far too short, but many more would follow, because they were now only an hour south of us. Sweet!

I was enrolled into Van Buren Junior High School, located only one block from our home. I remember enjoying my time there as a ninth grader very much. I made a few friends and the hours of separation from my new family was, I think, therapeutic for all of us. I went back to being academically average and fit in with the average kids. I attended my first school dance that year and watched the very first space shuttle launch from our second floor home room balcony. On the weekends, I mowed lawns for extra money to buy school clothes and was, in fact, living a pretty average teenage life. It would also be the year that I discovered, to the chagrin of everyone within a block of our home, that I was a natural drummer. So with a little prodding, Dad and Paula allowed me to sign up for a beginners drum class at school that year. I excelled at those lessons and was subsequently recommended by my teacher to the high school marching band the following school year. This was an uncommon recommendation. Most kids my age needed at least a few years of preparation before being asked to march with the high school band. So I knew very well what an honor this recommendation was. I then received an invitation letter to attend the summer band camp held at the high school. This came just prior to my sophomore year and all of this news had me brimming with new excitement.

It also came on the heels of a second tumultuous summer in our little household; one that markedly resembled the summer before. So once again, time outside of the home was, at least in my estimation, a good thing for everyone. During the camp, I made the cut for the drum line and looked forward to the coming school year. We all endured (and I don't use that word lightly) the few remaining weeks of that summer together until finally the big day arrived and we were on the school bus headed across town to Hillsborough High School. As the bus rolled up to the front of that huge school we were completely intimidated. Oh, we would never have told you that then, but we were terrified. That place took up three city blocks and had nearly twenty five hundred students running around. We were only sophomores and those high school kids were just so big. In fact, everything about that big, beautiful place made us feel small. It was an antique of a building; two-story brick with a giant clock tower right in the center. It was much more reminiscent of some New England style university or perhaps something out of Nineteenth Century London. But like everything else, we adjusted and in no time were actually feeling very much at home there.

The greatest thing about a large school is that a few of you can easily stick together and hide in the crowd. This would be my strategy throughout my sophomore year. Now, just because I made the drum line in the "Big Red" marching band did not mean that I would soon be marching with a snare drum strapped around my neck. I was still only a sophomore. I would have to pay my dues and climb the same ladder that all of the drummers who had come before me had climbed. I would have to start at the bottom and work my way up to that coveted snare line. That meant I would be on the cymbals for a little while. But I didn't mind. In fact, I loved it. I learned every cool move that I could with those things and enjoyed every minute marching with those kids. When we marched out of those enclosed hallways for a Friday night football game, with the deafening noise of our drums echoing off every wall in the school, the crowd would just lose their minds. We literally possessed the power to make the entire stadium dance and, for a few fleeting moments, we were stars.

I worked very hard that year until I had finally eliminated all competition and secure for myself a position on the snare line. I had literally learned how to produce a flawless drum roll on a pillow, never bouncing the tip of a stick. Anyone who knows anything about drum rolls knows how nearly impossible it is to accomplish a roll without bouncing the sticks. I so impressed the seniors on the line that my acceptance into their inner circle of friendship was also secured. That doesn't mean anything to me now, but as a sixteen year old sophomore, it meant everything.

Then, in February of 1982, I reached the pinnacle of my drum line experience. The "Big Red" band was to march in the annual Gasparilla parade in downtown Tampa. I never felt or looked so good in my life. We wore shiny black parachute pants and a glistening white tuxedo shirt with a black bow tie. We all looked like something out of a Michael Jackson video and we had the moves to match, spinning and clicking our sticks as we marched and played. We even learned to simultaneously throw our sticks to the ground, causing them to bounce off of the pavement and back into our hands. What a cool move that was. I felt as though I had accomplished everything that I could have accomplished there and was feeling very pleased with myself indeed. At that moment, I felt more removed from my torturous childhood than ever before. But I was also completely blind to the accumulating frustration that was building inside my dad and stepmom. While I was enjoying my sophomore year of high school, they were literally bracing themselves for the coming summer. They had never really counted the cost of bringing two totally damaged boys into their lives and were now quickly coming to the conclusion that it was no longer worth the fight. Other options were being considered and our future with that family was essentially being thrown into question. I'm certain that their motives were not evil. It was likely the only way they knew to salvage their family and move on with some sense of normalcy.

Unbeknownst to me, toward the end of that school year a plan was being put into play. It seemed that Dad and Paula, having had quite enough of this drama, had discovered a way to rid themselves of my presence for the summer--and quite possibly for good. There was a large tobacco farm in Connecticut that offered summer employment for high school students. Actually, it wouldn't surprise me if it is still there. It was kind of a summer camp, but one where the kids actually earned money. The arrangement was this. The owners of that farm, after receiving my application and approving my employment, would charter several large buses and transport nearly two hundred kids from Tampa, Florida to Connecticut. We would live in large dormitories and would receive three great meals a day. We would then work in the tobacco fields from morning to evening on weekdays and would rest on the weekends. All of our work hours were carefully recorded and all earned monies were banked until the day we departed. Small cash allowances would be made for some minor weekend spending, but for the most part, our money was banked. This would assure that each student would return home with nearly two thousand dollars of hard earned summer cash. The theory was that since the kids had worked so hard for this money, they would be very careful in the spending of it. At the end of the summer, the company would bus the children back to their waiting families as better citizens because of the experience. In my mind, it was a free ride to a strange new place, with no parent looking over my shoulder. What kid would pass that up? The promise of riches only sweetened the deal and so I jumped at the opportunity. Dad and Paula were extremely supportive of this venture and seemed every bit as excited as I was. Now I know why.

CHAPTER EIGHT

PICKING UP THE PIECES

THE SCHOOL YEAR ENDED AND I was to be a junior the following year. Not many days, later I was dropped off at the Grey Hound bus station in downtown Tampa. There I, along with nearly two hundred other kids, boarded three waiting buses and departed for New England. It took us nearly two full days to make the fifteen hundred mile journey and the loneliness set in immediately. I did not know anyone in that entire group and that was not a good thing. Teenagers have an ominous reputation for not being particularly warm towards other teenagers who are strangers to them. This only added to the loneliness. I longed to receive a letter or a phone call from Dad, telling me that even though things were stormy at home, we would find a way to get through it. But no letter came. As a matter of fact, I do not remember a single communication from Dad or Paula the entire time I was away. My mother, on the other hand, never stopped writing and taking my collect phone calls. This is what sustained me through that long, laborious summer. As far as the climate was concerned, Connecticut was a particularly strange place indeed, at least for a Florida boy. The days in the fields were tortuously hot and sweaty, while many of the nights would find the temperature dipping to near freezing. It was like a cruel joke. It was as if Old Man Winter and Old Man Summer were in a sick contest to see who could kill us first.

Eventually, I made a few friends, collected a few memories and saw this summer's adventure come to its conclusion. I was very eager to return to my home in sunny central Florida and prepare for my junior year of high school. It was a long ride home, but had I known what was waiting for me, I would have wished it longer. We arrived at downtown Tampa as the sun was setting. Those few familiar skyscrapers seemed to be warmly welcoming me home. Unfortunately for me, that would be the extent of the warm welcomes. We pulled into the Grey Hound station from whence we had so eagerly departed a few months prior and I steadfastly scanned the crowd for a glimpse of my smiling family. They would certainly be waiting to hug me and take me home to a hot meal and plenty of conversation. But there was to be no such reunion. I scanned until I strained my eyes to tears and never found them. I concluded that they were running behind and that with a little patience I would soon spot their car pulling in. I stood and watched as each of my companions was eagerly scooped up by their loved ones, until I alone was left there waiting. I waited and waited until the last of the sunlight had faded away as quickly as my friends had vanished. It was now becoming dark and I was becoming more than a little concerned. Had they forgotten that today was the day? I innocently placed a dime into the pay phone and called home. What followed was a truly sad event.

One of the kids answered the phone and I said "Hey is mom or dad there?" Eli and I had become accustomed to calling Paula "mom" during that year and a half. A few seconds later, Paula picked up the phone and said "Yes, Jimmy." I said "Hi, I'm home." I was really expecting to hear her say "Oh no, we forgot you baby. Hold on. We'll be there soon." But to my horror she instead responded "Okay, what would you like us to do about it?" I didn't know if she was kidding or what, so with a half-smile on my face I said "No, ma'am, I mean I'm downtown at the bus station." The horror solidified its grip on me when she responded "I heard you, Jimmy; what do you want?" She sounded pretty angry for someone who had not seen or spoken to me in more than three months. So I sheepishly asked "May I speak to Dad?" With a deep sigh of frustration, she said "Hold on." Again the phone was abandoned, but this time the wait seemed like forever. Finally, Paula picked it up again and said "Your dad is working on a car and cannot come to the phone." With a little more panic in my voice I asked, "Does he know that I am at the bus station?" Without missing a beat she delivered the death blow. "Yes, he knows. Goodbye,

Jimmy." Click. My heart sank as I realized what had just happened. I was abandoned. With one abbreviated phone conversation and a well-timed hang up, they had effectively washed their hands of me. The anger, sadness and fear immediately overwhelmed me and I began to sob. How could this be happening? After all that I had survived, was I now to be simply spat out onto the streets like a some undesirable chewed up piece of rubbish? I felt utterly alone. I felt like an orphan. I was in shock for a little while and literally had no idea what to do. I sat there in that big empty room for what seemed like an eternity. I literally had no idea what to do next. I had no money with me since the few dollars that I had begun my journey with had run out days ago and the money that I had just earned in Connecticut was being mailed to my dad's house. Besides, I would have had no idea what to do with it even if I did have it. I would have certainly been taken advantage of or conned out of it almost immediately. So it was actually better that I had nothing with me. I had heard stories about other kids who had been kicked out of their homes and were forced to live on the streets, but I had no such street skills. There was no way that I was going to survive out there on my own like that. I was certain that I would be robbed or killed within the first twenty-four hours. The truth is I wouldn't have even lasted twenty-four minutes out there. All of these thoughts were swirling around in my head. I thought to myself "Dear God, what am I supposed to do now?" I thought of calling the police, but I remembered that in sixteen years no branch of any government had been able to help me, not even the police. Besides, their presence would only attract unwanted attention to me--and unwanted attention was the last thing that I needed. I was doing my very best to remain hidden in plain sight. I was sixteen years old, five foot two inches tall, 105 lbs and was all alone. I was in serious trouble and I knew it.

I began to rummage through my wallet to see if I could find a few dollars for some food, as hunger was creeping in on me once again. While searching, I came across the business card of one of those court appointed councilors that we had spent some time with the previous year. I had forgotten that it was in my wallet, but I know now that God had led me to tuck it in there months ago, in preparation for this very night. I called the man and recounted every thing that had just happened to me. He kindly dropped whatever it was that he was doing and raced over to the bus station. He was utterly astonished at what my dad had just done. I think he called them, out of some sense of disbelief and they confirmed the story. As he stood there rubbing his forehead he hung up the phone, took a deep breath and asked me if I was hungry. While he watched me scarf down a hamburger, I began to see the wheels spinning in his head. I could tell that he had no idea what to do with me. Instead of telling me what the next step would be, he actually asked me if I knew anyone that I could live with. I could not believe my ears. This guy could not get the mighty wheels of justice rolling back in that court room a year ago when I had first told him about the years of abuse and now he couldn't even find me a safe place to sleep. I didn't know if my government was actually that incompetent or if this fellow was simply refusing to live up to his résumé. I thought about it while I finished my meal and finally said "I don't know. Maybe I can stay with my friend Anthony."

Anthony was actually Antonio Ortiz. I had met this young man nearly two years prior during my time at Van Buren Junior High School. We had become as good friends as two sixteen-year-old boys could be and his family liked me. His parents were a very kind hearted working class couple who immediately sympathized with my predicament and agreed to allow me to live with them. I was too young to understand the huge sacrifice that these two saints were signing up for. They weren't rich. On the contrary, they had to work very hard to provide for Anthony and his two younger brothers. Now they would have yet another hungry teenage mouth to feed and they did so without ever raising a word of complaint. They immediately took me into their home and treated me as one of there own children. They never complained about my being there. Eventually, Anthony's younger brothers began to feel the strain of some new kid living in their space and the tension began to mount between us. My stay with that beautiful family lasted nearly two months, which allowed me just enough time to begin my junior year of high school with some sense of normalcy. But as the frustration continued to build between me and the two younger boys, I thought it best to try and live with another friend. I put in a call to another pal from Junior High School, Gil "Junior" Florez and asked him if I could come and stay with him. He asked his parents, who were also a saintly working class couple from our neighborhood. They knew that they were in no position to raise someone else's teenager. So they very carefully thought through their answer before agreeing to allow me to stay for a few days until I could make a more suitable arrangement. I left Anthony's house thinking what a great family they were and wished that I could have grown up in a home like theirs.

I did spend the next few days in the Florez home and was made to feel every bit as at home as the Ortiz family had made me feel. I used that time wisely and attempted to broker a new living situation with the family of a third friend. I was successful again finding sympathy in the eyes of strangers. I did not know him and his parents nearly as well as I knew the first two families and have since forgotten their last name. My friend's name was Mark and he lived with his mother and his stepfather. I remember that the stepfather's first name was Fred. He was an elderly, ex-military man. I do not remember His wife's name because he kept calling her "Cap-Com." He refused to call me Jim and instead chose to address me as "P.F.C." He knew that I was in fact a Staff Sergeant in my high school's J.R.O.T.C. program, yet he insisted on P.F.C. For all of you who may not know what those letters stand for, it is an abbreviation for Private First Class. He, being a constant jokester, had effectively demoted me. But I never minded it as it was always said in fun. Even though this couple was working very hard just to keep a roof over their own heads, they were as kind to me as the other two families had been. I was not at all picky or ungrateful and found their couch a very comfortable place to sleep. Their old house was actually within walking distance of my high school. I found this to be quite convenient indeed since my only goal in life at that time, besides eating every day, was to finish high school. But finishing high school with my peers would prove to be a nearly impossible dream.

It was now going on nearly seven months, including my summer in Connecticut, with no real family structure. The money that I had earned in Connecticut had finally arrived at my dad's house in the form of a check for sixteen hundred dollars. I went to Dad's house and picked up the check. He told me my other belongings had been boxed up and that I could take them. I took my money and my boxes and lingered for a moment or two hoping for an invitation to return home. But none came, so I put on my tough new face and walked away. There is no way to describe the pain that accompanies that kind of total rejection. But I soon cheered up, having the good fortune of finding a bank that would cash my check. Yes, you heard me correctly. I said they cashed it. I can already hear your collective groans as I type these words. And you know very well what happened next. With every ounce of wisdom and life skills that I had acquired over my long sixteen years of life, I took that money straight to the mall and spent almost all of it in one glorious frenzy. Nearly thirteen hundred dollars were wisely spent on fashionable clothes that were currently in style, but probably would not be the following week. The rest was spent on mall food, movies, novelties and an expensive cab ride to and from the mall. Within a few days, I was completely broke. Ah, a fool and his money.

The following week I found myself sitting in the school cafeteria sporting my fine new threads, wishing that I had a dollar and a half to purchase a school lunch. Hunger has a way of suppressing pride and if I intended to eat that day, I was going to have to swallow mine and get creative. I snuck back into the kitchen and asked the school lunch ladies if they would allow me to work in the kitchen for a lunch. They informed me that, although they were sorry, they were not authorized to allow such a thing. So that day I was to go hungry. Yes, I know--I bloody well deserved it. As you can imagine, my eighty dollar pants mocked me for the balance of the afternoon. I felt like eating them.

I guess those nice lunch ladies actually felt sorry enough for me to report my offer of "Will work for food" to the Dean's office. During one of my last periods of class that day, with my stomach now chewing on my ribs, one of the school resource councilors came to my class room and asked the teacher if I could be excused for the remainder of the class. I was escorted to his office and asked about the incident in the cafeteria. I didn't dare tell him about my big adventure at the mall a few days prior, for fear that he would club me over the head with his paddle and send me out to face the music. I explained that I had no money and was merely finding a way to earn a lunch. With much compassion, he told me that I would never have that problem again for the remainder of the year. He signed me up for the school's free lunch program. I was as happy as a kid on Christmas morning. He then asked me about my home life. When I explained my current situation he took me to the school's food bank and loaded up a couple of boxes of groceries. I knew that Fred and Cap-Com would be thrilled. Thanksgiving was quickly approaching and this nice man included a large turkey and all the fixings. Because of his kindness, we enjoyed a great Thanksgiving meal and I never missed another lunch at school. I still deserved a beating for that mall thing, though.

Now that food was no longer an issue, I could concentrate on the goal of finishing high school. I am living proof that it takes an extremely gifted and self motivated teenager to finish high school on his own without any family or real positive outside influence. I know this because it only took a few short weeks for me and my grades to begin to plummet toward failure. I was truly alone in the world and felt as though no one believed in me. I was exhausted from the continual labor of suppressing the memory of my childhood and the constant weight of the whole world which was now resting squarely on my shoulders. I was too young to be this tired. I lost almost every night of sleep for the next little while contemplating where my life was headed. It seemed that no matter how badly I wanted to finish school, it was not going to be in the cards for me. Failure seemed imminent.

I didn't know it at the time, but Eli had received the same ousting that I had received from Dad and Paula. He had not taken any out of state summer trip like I had, but was simply admitted to a mental hospital to be evaluated for mental illness. Once it had been determined that he had no mental deficiencies, Dad and Paula were contacted and told to take him home. Eli later told me that the doctor who had been testing him actually considered reporting the case to the authorities, but never did. Instead, it would be easier to simply once again push him and the whole ugly matter away. Dad and Paula were not going to be so easily deterred from procuring other living arrangements for Eli and immediately set their eyes on a boy's home somewhere in the area. They talked it up and tried to sell Eli on the whole thing, but what were they expecting him to say? He knew that he was being sent away. This whole boy's home thing was actually going to cost Dad and Paula some money and just prior to Eli going, they changed their minds. He was told that he would instead have to return to live with Devlin and our mother down in Sarasota. Nice. I was too busy surviving out there on my own to even know that he was already back under their roof.

As long as school was in session, I could count on at least one hot meal every day. But Christmas break soon arrived and a whole new problem presented itself. While all of the other kids ran off cheering, I slowly walked back to my friend's little house knowing that my food source had just run out. It was the emptiest Christmas I had ever known. At least as a child I had my brothers and sisters. It didn't take long for the hunger to set in and I was not sure where my next meal would come from or when for that matter. It was becoming clear that I was not going to be able to survive on my own like this much longer. But I was now out of friends and with my options all gone and my stomach continually growling, I did what any sixteen-year-old kid in my position would do. I called my mother.

No matter what happens in life, you can be sure that most mothers never stop caring. Devlin was still as stingy as he was greedy and my mom never really had any money on her, but some how she scraped together enough money that morning to drive the fifty miles to rescue her son. I remember that it was a particularly cold December morning, at least for central Florida. We arranged to meet at a park where we usually met for visitations. As I waited, I shivered, but the anticipated meal kept hope alive. Finally after hours of waiting, I saw that old tan Cadillac come lumbering into the park and, once again, I felt saved. The warm car, the happy faces and a short ride to some hot food made all of the difference in the world. Soon we were on our way to mom's house in Sarasota, where she still lived with Devlin.

Certain other events which had occurred at Devlin and mom's house while I was living with my dad, had established a set of "strict" rules which governed such visits. I think that during the time that we were going through the custody hearings in Tampa, someone had called the Florida abuse hotline to report concerns of child abuse and molestation which may still have been occurring to the remaining children. Although their concerns were certainly justified, once again nothing would be done to bring an end to this fellow's reign of terror. Right after the custody issue had been resolved with Eli and me, the state agency which was then known as H.R.S. went to the schools of Nathan, Rebecca, Sarah and Carson and took custody of them while they investigated these recent allegations. The kids lived in some shelter and had limited supervised visits with mom and no contact with Devlin. Devlin was the first to be informed about the actions taken by H.R.S. Mom had no idea what had occurred until Devlin came running into their house in a panic. He told her, as he grabbed a few of his belongings that he was going out the back door, getting on his boat and leaving. She asked him what in the world was going on and where he was going. He told her that he was pretty sure that the authorities would be arriving soon and all of her questions would be answered. Mom, who was now left there alone, was soon contacted and informed of what had taken place concerning the kids. She nearly fell apart. The children had been removed and an inquiry would soon follow. It did, but somehow their joke of an investigation concluded that Devlin and the kids needed psychological intervention and that the kids would be allowed to return home to again live with him.

This was now the third time that a state government had gotten involved in the ordeal and failed to bring this child rapist to justice. I'm not trying to be unreasonable and believe me I know how difficult these child abuse investigations can be, especially in developing probable cause for an arrest. But I don't think that these people were even trying. Investigators know that they must treat each allegation and investigation with the same tenacity, believing that the allegation may very well be true; even though many are not. Investigatory problems arise when some case workers and law enforcement officers grow increasingly skeptical and lethargic in their efforts to find the truth. I think that this reoccurring phenomenon arises out of the investigators frustration in a couple of areas. The first usually comes on the heels of a laborious investigation which yields up the appropriate evidence for a conviction of an offender. It becomes particularly frustrating when the investigation is crowned with a confession from that perpetrator. Prior to the case ever entering a court room, a deal is struck between the bad guy and the Prosecuting Attorney's Office in an attempt to avoid a costly, drawn out trial. In exchange for their guilty plea, the perpetrator often receives much less prison time than the law would otherwise demand and with it the hope of a future parole and probation period. Just like that, a convicted offender has hope of one day going home and, just like that, future victims are at risk. This is not the case every time, but it only takes a few of these to literally cost some children their lives--and to make some investigators wonder why they even tried.

A second area of frustration develops over time after a number of investigations expose more lies than evidence. Discovering well into an investigation that the alleged victim had in fact been deceiving the investigators has an unfortunate consequence, given enough time, of watering down subsequent investigations. It is extremely imperative that investigating agencies not allow these setbacks to govern their future diligence. It is equally imperative that our citizenry begin to reassert their ownership of *their* judicial centers and *their* legislative capitols. Elected officials simply must be told what is expected of them and held accountable for their actions. They are not and never have been the boss. They merely represent their boss (the people). In my opinion, it's high time that the true boss take ownership and responsibility of their government, even if it means firing some of their employees. I know that sounds extreme, but our form of government only works when the people are engaged. Otherwise, the politicians and the judges feel tempted to cater to their own interests, or merely represent themselves, or just make it up as they go. Or worse yet, they will sell themselves out to the highest bidders; which seems to be the most popular of the temptations. Subsequently, we are seeing many parts of our society feeling left out and disenfranchised by the government that had at one time represented them. Now as unfortunate as it is, this is largely our own fault. The number of people who stay home on Election Day is appalling. These things which tend to perplex us so greatly in this land will never change unless we step up to the responsibility that has been given to us in the running of our country. What is desperately needed at this time is a great shaking loose, an awaking if you will, of the American people; that is if they don't wish to see their great country slip quietly off into obscurity. Wake up my brothers and sisters! Your country and your children, who are the very future of your country, are in peril. While we take our ease and give little attention to the goings-on in the halls of power, sinister forces are creeping in, threatening to take away our land--one freedom and one child at a time. Arise, you mighty American! Let them hear you roar from the ballot boxes and take back what your employees have usurped from you.

Well, back to our story. One of the new rules that Devlin had been given was that if Eli or I came to Sarasota to visit our mother, he would have to vacate the home until we were gone. He complied every time with that rule and, although I had no idea where he would go, I never saw him when I visited.

This particular visit was a bit more extended than previous visits since school was out and I really had nothing to return to anyway. While I was there in Sarasota, I met a few new friends who began to join forces with my mom in an attempt to convince me to change high schools and move to Sarasota. This was indeed a most difficult decision. On the one hand, I had no real home or means of support for myself in Tampa. On the other hand, I could not stomach the prospect of again having to live in the same house with Devlin. But at that moment, these appeared to be my only two options. Mom tried to reassure me that the past was behind us and that nothing bad would ever happen to me again. She told me that she and Devlin had already discussed the possibility of my return and that Devlin was far too afraid to ever try anything bad again. She tried to console me with the knowledge that Eli had already returned to live with them and that nothing bad had happened to him. I knew that I was now too old and too big to ever allow Devlin to attack or molest me again and, although it may sound grotesque, it was actually the better of the two choices if I intended to survive. There was no one to discuss it with, so I made the decision to move back to mom's house. After a quick journey to Tampa to pack my meager belongings, the deal was done.

I guess I couldn't just expect Devlin to stay away from his home forever now that I was living there also, although that would have been great. I'd be lying if I said I wasn't constantly wishing that he would simply disappear. Frankly, I didn't care how either. Abandon the family, die—heck, at the time it would not have bothered me a bit if he had suddenly found himself overcome with guilt and killed himself. I know that sounds terrible, but give me a break here. My mind was bursting with all of those god-awful memories and the man who put them all there was standing in the kitchen sipping hot tea. I had to see him and remember every terrible detail every day. Was I angry? You bet I was angry. I was sixteen and penniless. I was so frustrated that I couldn't see straight and there wasn't a thing that I could do about it. All I could think about was the day that this bum would be out of my life forever. So excuse me if I don't sound too tearful about the prospects of his demise. Why wouldn't he just die? It didn't seem too unfair to wish such a thing on such a bad person. Unfortunately I would have to wait a little longer, because he did return and once again I found myself living with a child predator. I don't think either one of us was happy about the deal. But there it was. We simply did our best to stay out of each other's way. It was a terribly awkward living arrangement trying to avoid all conversation and eye contact with another member of the household like that. But what in the world were we supposed to do--just pretend the past decade never happened? We both knew it did and it just sucked that we had to live there together. This was a tragic testament to the utter impotence of the current political system. I mean my God, how did it ever come back to this?

Well, now that I was there, I had to be enrolled into Sarasota High School, where I would finish my junior year. My real trouble there began almost immediately when I realized that the only clothes that I had to my name were those stupid Michael Jackson costumes that I had spent nearly thirteen hundred dollars on six months earlier. These had all fallen out of favor months ago and, believe me, the kids at my new school wasted little time and showed no mercy in letting me know about it. Neither mom nor I had any money for any newer, more conservative school clothes, so I simply had to tough out the rest of the year with what I had. And the hits keep coming.

I was only back at Devlin's house for a few weeks when he and mom had some horrendous argument in the middle of the night about a new job that she had just taken. They got ridiculously loud for a while before she barged into my room and said "Pack your things. We're leaving." I thought to myself: here we go again; will this insanity never end? I had no idea where she thought that we might be going at that hour, but Eli, Sarah, Carson and I all grabbed a few things and off we drove into the night. After she calmed down a bit, we had to face the reality that we were nearly broke and had no place to go. We scrounged up around twenty dollars between us and crashed in some cheap motel for the night. Ever notice that when you're really down and tired, checkout time seems to come awfully fast? Well, it did and that was the end of the money. It was beginning to appear that we were going to be genuinely homeless and have to live in the car. Hunger also comes fast when food is not available and as her children began asking for something to eat; my mother became very sad indeed. Real despair has a creepy way of gathering its own horrible momentum. Our pride usually prevents us from seeking it, but without help you can get yourself stuck in its powerful rip current for a long time. We had no such intentions, so we all swallowed our pride and prayed for help. We then started asking people for help and, thank God, our prayers were answered and help did arrive later that afternoon. It came in the form of a local Assemblies of God minister and his wife, the leaders of the church that mom had been attending. They were sympathetic to our plight and allowed us to sleep in the church until we could make more permanent arrangements for ourselves. We only had to sleep there one night before mom's new boss and his family decided to allow us to stay with them until we could secure an apartment. Life was changing fast for us again and, as usual, God was sending the right help at the right time. Sometimes that help came in very strange ways indeed, but it always came. Take mom's boss, for instance. This guy had a huge crush on her, which is probably what she and Devlin were arguing about the night we left. This little schoolboy crush of his worked greatly to our advantage because his heart got the better of his brain and he could not resist the urge to pay for our first months rent in a duplex. Right on, God! Even though it was in a very poor neighborhood and a rough one at that, we were thrilled. At long last we had a place of our own to call home.

For the first time in my mom's adult life, she was working and supporting a family. She worked for this guy as a secretary at his storage yard and money was very tight for the next few months. This guy was married, but was making open passes at my mom nonstop. He even bought her a car. Well, he bought himself a car that she liked very much and as a "gift," he let her take it home and drive it as much as she wanted to. My mom was not interested in this guy romantically, but he simply was not getting the hint. Some guys just have to learn things the hard way, I guess. Anyway, it all finally ended with him in one explosive scene in our front yard late one night. And when I say explosive, um, yeah, he most definitely got the message that night. It all went down like this. He told my mom that he and his wife were going out on his boat for a ride that evening. He told her that they wanted to invite her along as well. She accepted only to discover at the dock that his wife was not going and, in fact had never been going. Mom changed her mind and I guess the guy had enough of her hard-to-get ways. He followed her back to our duplex, invited himself in and started arguing with her. I came out of my room and asked them to keep it down because I had school the next day and all the kids were sleeping. I was also beginning to reach my boiling point with these childish late-night shouting matches. I think they saw the seriousness in my face. They agreed to be quiet and take their little spat out to the front yard. The next thing I remember was Eli yelling for me to get out there. I looked out of my bedroom window and saw this guy punch my mom in the face, while holding her throat in his other hand. Oh hell no! Those days are over, my friend! I grabbed my twenty gage shotgun and walked out the front door with it. I guess he was too engrossed in his little fight, because the sight of my very large gun didn't seem to adequately arrest his attention or impress him as I would have liked it to. Like I said some guys just have to feel the pinch first. Anyway, like an idiot he just kept struggling with mom. I let him hear that awful heart-gripping, pants-wetting "chink chink" of me racking one into the chamber, but still this moron seemed to not fully grasp what was about to happen to him and actually drew his fist back to hit mom again. Man, this dude must be retarded or something, because the sound of that round being chambered for action usually causes people to pass out. I decided to quit messing around with this dumb ass and blasted one off into the air. I was only about ten feet from him and the thunderous explosion shook him to his core. That did the trick. I then pointed the gun at him directly and racked another one into the chamber. He heard that one. I could literally see his knees shaking as he frantically waved both hands from right to left in an attempt to get me to point that cannon elsewhere. He stuttered and tried to say something to me, but couldn't get anything coherent out. I, on the other hand, was thinking very clearly, so I said to him, "I think it's time for you to go now." He jumped into his truck and drove off screaming something about calling the police, but I never saw him again after that night.

Mom took a new job soon after that with the state of Florida's financial assistance and food stamp office in Sarasota. It was just enough to keep us floating while I finished my junior year. When summer time came, I determined that I would never be broke again if I could help it. I took a day job and an evening job and did what I could to help mom. I also enjoyed spoiling Carson, who was now seven years old. I would take him on cross-town bus rides and lavish gifts on him at the mall. I was making around two hundred dollars a week between the two jobs. For the average seventeen-year-old in 1984, that was a lot of stinking money. Unfortunately, I had still obviously learned nothing about money management, as I found it quite easy to spend those two hundred dollars every week. I did, however, remember my hard lesson in fashion choice from the previous year and entered what was probably the most conservative time of my life in regards to my wardrobe.

The inner pain began.

As the summer of '84 came to an end, I was spending nearly every day hiding from the world at the movie cinema. I was a real movie hound back then and there was never any shortage of decent flicks to enjoy. I think I saw "Ghost Busters" twenty times that summer. Only a new school year had the power to break the monotony and pry me out of that theater seat. So back to Sarasota High School I went.

I had to quit my day job, but I hung on to my evening job. I probably shouldn't admit this to you, but I was a real live telephone solicitor. Yes, I probably interrupted your dinner a time or two. Sorry about that. I was actually being paid a commission to raise money for the "Police Benevolent Association". Although the work took some getting used to, I actually raised a good deal of money for that organization. I had always been a keen observer of human behavior, so it didn't take me very long to realize that there were only two kinds of salesmen in that office: those who were making money and those who were not. I told myself that if I wanted to make money, I would have to imitate the money makers. I listened closely to the way they changed their voice to sound like radio announcers and to the ridiculous crap that they were saying to those people at the other end of the line as if they had known them forever. I quickly became one of them and began to sell like there was no tomorrow. We had to be good, because what we were selling was an utterly useless "booster membership" which had no real value or benefit for the customer. For $25.00, we sent you a ten cent sticker for your car and a thank you note. Now don't get me wrong. The P.B.A. is a very legitimate organization which has benefitted law enforcement officers for a long time, but I think I would have felt better just asking them for their money. Oh, well, I'm sure all those kind folks must have experienced something of their own noble feelings for contributing to what they perceived was a worthy cause. It's just that getting them to do it was never an easy task so we had to Sell! Sell! Sell! Ironically, given my own boat load of baggage, the tremendous rejection that accompanies that line of work didn't bother me. I knew very well that it was a numbers game and that the more people I called the more sales I would make. I did well and the general manager took notice. He called me in for a meeting and told me that if I could get to work right after school, I could join the half day sales team. They were the same guys that I worked with at night, but were there all day. More hours meant more money, so I immediately took him up on his offer and continued to do well.

I was eighteen years old now and while, most other eighteen year olds were trying out their new adult wings and taking flight, I was entering what would possibly be the darkest chapter of my adult life. For at precisely that moment, I became acutely aware of a relentless inner pain which mercilessly vexed me day and night. Sometimes it was just a minor irritation, but other times, not so minor More often than not, it would fully manifest itself in a dizzying array of mental images which would literally interrupt my life and could often last for days. It was such a heavy feeling of significant failure and worthlessness, accentuated by utter humiliation. I think it had actually been there all along, but had finally reached the point where I could no longer ignore it. My life was quickly beginning to feel like a total loss. I was too young and ignorant to realize that it was just my childhood revisiting me and even if I could have known it, I was still powerless to mend it. So I did what I thought anyone else would have done in my anguish. I began a diligent search for any tonic or remedy which might prove useful in the silencing of those inner demons. Cue the saloon music.

All of the guys that I worked with were ten to fifteen years older than me. My acceptance into their inner circle opened a whole new world of self-medication and I began to spend as much time with them as I could. Now young guys seldom influence the older and, as you may have already guessed, it didn't take very long for me to begin to pick up some of their bad habits, especially drunkenness. Those guys loved to be drunk. When they weren't working, it seemed like they were thoroughly enjoying their lives and that's what I wanted as well. Again, I was simply too young to realize that they were all just a bunch of socially pleasant alcoholics, but at age eighteen I discovered that their alcohol had a profound ability to dull my inner pain, at least for a little while. I don't know, maybe it was the perpetrator who had never been brought to justice, or maybe it was the lost childhood. Perhaps it was all of those rapes, beatings and threats that were still right there in the back of my mind, replaying themselves again and again in full Technicolor. Whatever it was, I had without a doubt discovered my medicine. Up to this point in my life, I had never drank any alcohol or taken any drugs of any kind. I was a pretty good kid considering what I had lived through. But all of that was about to change and I was about to take a walk on the wild side.

Now that I think about it, I'm sure that my other siblings were also experiencing something of the same inner turmoil which was clearly evidenced by the emotional shipwrecks that we had all become. Tragically, I began to slip away from my once fiery faith and found myself spending the lion's share of my time trying to fix the pain rather than seeking my God. Eli and I had also begun to drift apart. We fought about everything. We were both hurting and were probably just frustrating each other with the different ways in which we were each trying to cope. I was content to be drunk and quiet, while he preferred getting high and listening to loud music in the house. This brought us into physical combat all the time. We finally became tired of the fighting and simply ignored each other for a couple of years. During those two years, I journeyed farther and farther down that dark road toward alcoholism, while he went down his own dark path of self-destruction.

At first, simply spending my weekends with the guys killing a keg of beer was enough. In truth, I never really liked beer and actually still don't. Can you believe that; a guy who doesn't like beer, unbelievable. But it's true, I just tolerated it because I liked being with those new friends of mine. And, of course, the absence of the pain while swimming in those deep euphoric pools of sweet intoxication was always the real benefit, however short-lived they may have been. So, like it or not, beer obviously had its uses and I found myself exploiting those uses more and more. Not too many months later, the dark plot thickened and I was introduced to real liquor. Most had the same effect on me as beer. I would drink until the room would spin like a top and then I would fall down and hurl my guts out before passing out. But then I discovered one brand of straight whiskey that I could drink as much as I liked with no ill side affects. I could literally drink this stuff until I passed out and it never made me sick. From that point on, if I was not at work, I was smashed. I hated crowds and did not like spending time with people that I didn't know. So I almost never went out to parties or clubbing or anything like that. I just needed to be medicated. Less than a year later, I was a full blown alcoholic. I was constantly shaking with "detox" tremors and had been reduced to the guy who could do nothing in life except hold out for his next round of drinks. Yep, I was that guy. I was even addicted to the sound of ice chinkeling around in my glass. How bad is that? Unfortunately, it didn't take very long for the alcohol to exacerbate my problems as well. The inner turmoil was faithfully returning to me every morning anyway, no matter how much I drank the night before. Only now, I would awaken to find him standing there by my bedside with his evil brother "Hangover" smiling at me as well. Now I needed medicine for both--and the whole thing just kept getting worse.

Apparently, that wasn't enough lunacy for my young life, so what happened next only seemed natural. I met another "friend" at our office. This guy wasn't nearly the alcoholic that the rest of us were, but still he seemed every bit as intoxicated as we were. In my endless search for strong medicine, I wondered what his secret was. One weekend, while we were all sitting around a keg and doing our best to send it home empty, this guy fired up some weed. This was a brand new deal for me and I wasn't real sure what to do with it. His secret was out, though. In my current state of mind, I couldn't just let it go without at least trying it, so I smoked with him a few times. I must admit that it did produce the same powerful relieving effect as my liquid companion; however its high wasn't nearly as enduring and, although I did smoke with him from time to time, I never really embraced it like he did. I preferred my drink.

All of this chemical debauchery was having an unfortunate effect on my attention at school. I was quickly losing interest once again. I was still excelling at work though and my boss, upon seeing my growing disinterest with school, pounced on the opportunity. He told me that where I was going, I would have no need of a high school diploma. He then asked me to consider dropping out of school and moving to Tampa with a few of the guys to open a new office. I would be a full-timer and would have the opportunity to make some "real money". At the time, it was a really tempting offer because I was really getting tired of hearing my mom complain about my frequent absence from school. I was always asking her to write excuse notes to get me into class after skipping the previous day due to being hung over again. She hated to see what I was doing to myself, but at least I was still in school. So she kept the notes coming and after a while, I even quit reading them. I would just hand them to my home room teacher and take my seat. One day, in the spirit of teaching me a lesson, she got me good. She wrote "Please excuse my son from being absent yesterday, as he is an alcoholic and has trouble getting out of bed". Yeah, we still laugh about that one.

But eventually I came to the conclusion that I no longer wanted to fight the inevitable. I don't know why I had resigned myself to the idea that I was not going to be allowed to graduate. Maybe it had something to do with credits, but whatever it was I decided that I was no longer interested in trying to finish school. I told my mom that after some careful consideration, I had decided to drop out and move to Tampa with the rest of the crew. She hated the idea, but I was now eighteen and was legally allowed to make these decisions for myself if I was so inclined. So instead of fighting me over it, she decided to let it go. She signed me out the next day and, within a few months I was to be on my way back to Tampa to seek my fortune. But just prior to my hopeful departure, tragedy once again came crashing into my life.

The death of a princess

Rebecca had confided in me years earlier that she not only knew about my dark secret, but was herself regularly falling victim to Devlin's molesting ways. We could never really talk about it much for fear of inadvertently getting the other killed, so we mostly kept quiet. I guess by the time she entered her late teens the constant trauma began to really take its toll on her. By her sixteenth birthday it was quite obvious that she was at war with her inner demons and it was also obvious that she wasn't winning. This was a real shame in that she was outwardly a very typical teenage girl. She was ten times smarter than her siblings and possessed loads of potential. Her extraordinarily long blond hair coupled with her soft beautiful features and brilliant smile made her the envy of many other girls. Her soft heart and kind ways made her popular with everyone else. She was a constant "A" student and she really should also have been a cheerleader or class president or something like that. She probably would have been if the circumstances in her life had lent themselves to a more normal childhood. Unfortunately she was now every bit as damaged as I was and appeared to be getting worse. I don't know if it's any harder for girls to cope with such personal violations than it is for guys. I have actually heard the opposite is true, but which ever it is, she was finding it particularly difficult to deal with it all. Here stood a young woman who was literally the image of grace and beauty who couldn't help feeling anything but ugly. Devlin had proven to her over the years that he loved no one but himself and that he actually felt nothing but contempt for the rest of us. Where he really succeeded in destroying her though was in making her hate herself. I guess she simply succumbed to the dread and hopelessness that she was feeling because in early January of 1985, she attempted to take her own life by ingesting a handful of pills. The attempt was discovered and she was rushed to the hospital. The doctors pumped her stomach and saved her life. After a few days of recovering, she apologized to all of us and assured us that she had been depressed, and that the suicide attempt was only a grasp for sympathy. We knew her to be a totally honest girl and had no reason to disbelieve her. But she was also very smart and was easily able to lull us all into a false sense of security. I sincerely wish that I would have known then what I know now. I would have been able to reach her. I would have been able to help her. But I was still too young and ignorant to have any real situational awareness. Later that same month, while we were all feeling nothing but optimism about her mental well being, she walked into Devlin's bedroom, picked up his .38 caliber pistol, made a quiet exit to the back yard and shot herself. This time there was simply nothing that the doctors could do. Just like that, she was gone. The little girl who had come into my life when she was only one year old and who had been my constant companion through out all of those terrible years had just left us. Numerous family members flooded the hospital and filled its halls with the thunderous sound of their pain. Outwardly, it appeared to be a typical suicide, but I knew that this kid had been flat out murdered from the inside out. I had not only lost my own childhood, but now I had just lost someone who I loved every bit as much as I loved myself. It wasn't fair. It really should have been Devlin lying on that hospital bed, not her. As the permanence of her death set in, I wept for days. She was my kid sister and we were going to need each other in the coming years. Why was she gone? Her departure knocked a hole in me that has remained unto this day. I should write a whole lot more about this, but it's simply too painful. I think I'll dedicate this book to her. I still miss you, kid.

God is not a crutch.

After having received an additional blow of that magnitude, I was now more determined than ever to get out of that town. Soon enough, the time arrived. I packed my car and moved to Tampa. Five of the company top guns moved to Tampa, where we opened the new branch office. I worked sixty hours a week and stayed drunk the rest of the time. I shared an apartment with one of the guys who had come from the Ft. Meyers office and we got along famously. We became like two brothers who were drawn together by our common affection for alcohol and, oh, how liberally the alcohol flowed. I now had a whole new set of pains to go along with the old ones and they all needed to be medicated. I lived there in Tampa for around a year and never did make my fortune. On the contrary, I consistently struggled financially. It seemed that my sales well had run dry. While the other guys continued to do well, I was no longer the salesman that I had been in Sarasota. I racked my brain trying to fix the problem, but it simply did not lend itself to explanation. Looking back on it now, I can see that God was obviously preparing to bring this dark chapter of my life to an end. I just didn't know it yet.

Soon it was October, 1985. I was nineteen years old and a total drunk. One day, while minding my own business, I received an invitation to some informal Halloween party planned for later that weekend. Perhaps it was out of sheer boredom, but in a decision which was certainly not in keeping with my natural unction to avoid such a gathering, I accepted. It was just a handful of some hippie throwback friends of a friend, who were getting together to smoke some pot and get drunk, so I fit right in with them anyway. As we loaded up the car and headed toward the party, I was in the back seat getting a head start on the drinking. But during that ride across town my life changed forever. About halfway to the party and from quite out of the blue, there came a very intense, sharp, cramping pain which shot up the bottom of my left arm from my wrist and proceeded straight across my chest. I dropped my Bourbon and Coke and doubled over clinching my shirt. My right hand gripped tighter and tighter, as if I were wrestling with the angel of death himself for possession of my soul. It felt as though someone had reached in between my ribs, grabbed a handful of my heart and veins and squeezed. The pain was intense, but before I had another moment to consider what was happening to me, the squeeze relented and suddenly it was just gone as though it had never been there. I sat up in my seat, my eyes now big as saucers and wondered in terror if he was going to come back and finish me off. I just stared out the window for a little bit and waited, but he never did return and, as you could imagine, I was no longer in the mood to party. The pain may have evaporated, but the terror of the thing remained fully with me for the balance of the evening. Once home from the party and not nearly as drunk as I would have been under normal circumstances, I knelt down at the end of my bed and acknowledged the truth. Life is very delicate and fragile and that very well might have been it for me tonight. To that end I prayed these words to God, while kneeling there. "Father, please forgive my foolishness. But I am not sure what to do here. I admit that I am terrified, but still I have no intention to stop drinking. It is all that I know that helps me feel better. Let me say one last thing, and I will stop talking. You are God and I am not. I know that you love me. If you have something better for me then you are going to have to bring me to it, because I am lost."

Less than a week later, I got into a stupid argument with the office manager at work and got fired. I kid you not. I was honestly just trying to win the argument, not get myself fired. But be that as it may, I was now out of a job. A few days later, I was packed and driving back to Sarasota to live with my mom again--and "lead me to it" He did. Despite the feelings of uncertainty which always seems to accompany unemployment, it did feel great to be heading home for the holidays. There is something medicinal about being among the faces and routines of the people who make you feel that your life really does matter. Christmas soon arrived and money was as tight as ever. That didn't matter though. In fact, that never seemed to matter to us as long as we were together. I had never assigned a monetary value to Christmas nor pressured anyone else to do so. It simply meant something else to me.

Among the few gifts that I had received on this particular Christmas was one that would become an important benchmark in my life. I've long forgotten who it was that actually gave it to me, but someone bought me a fifth of my favorite brand of bourbon wrapped in a red ribbon. This was not at all an inappropriate gift for me considering my previous two years of extreme alcoholism and I accepted it gladly. I remember setting the bottle on top of an old piano that my mom had in her living room and would just stare at it as if it was the best gift I had received that year. My plan was to savor it with my eyes for a few days, and then drink it down once the pain returned. Well, it just sat there. I must have forgotten about it for a while because, as I remember it, the pain never did return. As a matter of fact, I wasn't even thinking about any pain or even about that illustrious bottle of pain medication, either. This was probably due to the fact that I had become altogether preoccupied with something else that was going on in the home. Yep, there's nothing like a sizable distraction to get your mind off of your own vices for a while. Anyway, I could not help but feel utterly amazed as I was witnessing some kind of a strange revival of faith or reconnection with God that mom and Sarah were obviously enjoying. I personally had abandoned all church going years ago, having found only old songs and soggy sermons about good behavior and religion. But something was definitely going on in mom and Sarah that was very different than anything I had ever seen before. Their eyes gleamed more brilliantly and their happiness was so genuine that I simply could not deny its authenticity. I actually found myself becoming somewhat envious of whatever it was that they had. They invited me time and again to go to church with them, but I was too used to refusing and soon they quit asking. But they never stopped praying for me. In truth, I think I was actually starving for what they had.

After a few months of wrestling with this perceived lack of theological common ground between my mother and me, my eyes were suddenly opened to a most astonishing revelation. One day, while sitting in mom's living room listening to some old record albums, I happen to glance at the top of her old piano. There I saw a dusty ribbon laden bottle of bourbon still setting where I had so carefully placed it months earlier. Had it really been that long? As my brain processed the implications of this astonishing scene, I turned my head, as if in slow motion, back toward the couch that I was sitting on. For a moment, I stared intently at my right hand, which was resting on the cushion next to me. I then slowly lifted that hand and held it out flat in front of my face. I was fully expecting to see what I had seen a hundred times before, but was quite pleased to observe the opposite. I really can't describe the relief that washed over me when I noticed that my hand was now as steady as a rock and was no longer trembling like a leaf in the wind. As a matter of fact, nothing in me was trembling. I should have started shaking weeks ago, yet everything in me was still and quiet. With the ghost of my recent past piping to me from atop that old piano, I glanced back in its direction with a confused look on my face. I remember saying to myself "Wow. I'm not really sure what's happening here, but what ever it is it's bigger than me and I'm not going to mess with it." And, just like, that my drinking days were behind me. It has now been more than twenty years and I have not had so much as a taste of alcohol. It was a miracle. It was an absolute answer to that little cry for help that I had whimpered to God months earlier, after that party. I had been given my life back and I was not about to be stupid or ungrateful.

Now in the telling of that part of my story, I have come across people who, in their stubborn refusal to believe in miracles, would politely dismiss out of hand the previous testimony. They would often say something like "Well, I don't know about miracles, but we all know that God helps those who help themselves." I really do wish that people would quit saying that. It's not at all helpful and is in fact quite unscriptural. The folks that are saying it have obviously never read the Bible for themselves and are simply repeating something that someone else had said. I mean it sounds pious and all, but it's simply not true. Had they just taken the time to read the thing for themselves, they would have discovered that those ridiculous lofty words are nowhere in the Book at all. God does not help those who help themselves; he rather helps those who can in no way help themselves. His entire story all the way through the Bible is one of him showing us that we cannot help or *save* ourselves and that he takes great delight and has gone to some considerable expense in rescuing his children whom he loves so dearly. God is no crutch my friend; he's more like a stretcher, as I would soon find out.

CHAPTER NINE

WELCOME HOME SON

AROUND AUGUST OF 1986, MOM approached me with yet another invitation to join her at church. I'm sure that it was mostly pride by this time, but I was still quite reluctant to go back to church. Apparently, there was to be a guest speaker this particular Sunday; an elderly woman whose name was Betty Baxter. She was coming to share her incredible story about how Jesus had literally touched and healed her crippled body when she was still a teenager. She had not stopped telling her story for the past fifty or sixty years and was now coming to mom's church to tell it again. All week, mom and her neighbor, who also went to the same church, pummeled me with invitations until finally I relented. I remember saying something brilliant to them in my usual condescending manner like "Okay, I'll go with you this Sunday if you will promise to quit asking me after that." She quickly accepted the deal and, although I did not know it then, my fate was sealed. From the very moment that I laid down that iron-like resistance, something strange began to happen to me. Emotions that had died in me years earlier began to quietly stir. My stubborn heart was suddenly wrapped in warmth as though I had just come in from a cold exile and found myself standing next to a large fire place ablaze with redemption. Like a pair of frostbitten feet that begin to tingle and feel the life and the blood coming back into them, so my soul began bursting with sensations that had been absent for years. God Almighty, I feel you again! I didn't fully grasp what was happening at that moment, but I felt completely at peace from the inside out. Years of ice and indifference began melting and all of that new water was finding its way out of my body through the holes in my eyes. At every turn, I could feel his love calling to me and the tears would just flow as my soul longed to find a way to respond to him.

Well, that Sunday arrived, and not a minute too soon. True to my word, I got up and started getting ready for church. This day was worse than the others in that I simply could not stop the tears. All the way there, I had to keep drying the water from my eyes. Hindsight being as informative as it is, I can now tell you what was happening to me. My spirit, which had been starved for years, was yearning for the love of its maker. And as the hour of worship approached, it wept with joy and anticipation. Mom's church was meeting in an office park and not a typical church building, which was a refreshing change from the stale religious backdrop that I had become accustomed to seeing and avoiding. I walked up to those double glass doors and pulled one open. As the air conditioning gushed out and hit me in the face, I felt The Lord Jesus himself envelop me in a great cosmic hug. The remaining ice quickly melted away as he whispered in an old familiar voice: "Welcome home, son. We've been expecting you. These people love you." If you think I was crying earlier, you should have seen that mess. But it was true; I honestly felt as though I had just crawled out of a cold grave and finally stumbled home. It was all so warm and inviting and it truly felt good to be among the living again. I was sad that I did not know the words to their songs, but as they sang to him I was singing with all of my heart on the inside.

Mrs. Baxter soon came to the platform and gave a stunning testimony of the healing that she had received decades earlier. But when she would address Jesus as "My Jesus," my heart would leap inside of me as my mind was instantly taken back with memories of that same Jesus in my childhood. What I said to myself is as clear now as it was the moment I thought it "I'm sure that when she finishes her speech, there will be some kind of invitation to come forward and pray. When that happens, I will be the first one there." Sure enough, she finished and the pastor of the church extended the invitation. I could not be held to my seat any longer and made a beeline to the altar. I do not remember who it was that met me there or what they may have said to me, but I remember what I said. "Father, my dear Father, you have the rest of my life if you want it. I will go anywhere or do anything that you wish for me." I never had to be invited to church again.

It was a most incredible awakening. It is simply amazing to remember just how dead and dull of hearing my spirit had become for all those years. And now, having spent those years wandering around in my own quiet wilderness, I have no problem understanding how another person can have trouble believing that God "spoke" to me. It is simply remarkable how deaf we humans can become to a God who loves us so much. But as remarkable as it sounds, it is true. So we look at another fellow who seems to be full of joy and peace and who is saying something a bit odd like "God spoke to me" and wonder why we can't hear him also. Then, instead of asking questions about our own spiritual well-being, we attack him as a fraud or a lunatic. It really comes down to a question of *choice*, doesn't it? If you choose to keep your distance from him and spend your life speculating about him, then your spirit will do the same thing that mine did. It will simply begin to lose its ability to see or hear him calling to you. Some have refused his advances for so long that their very consciences have died and they no longer care at all about him. The deepest tragedy of the human condition is that some will actually grow so entirely deaf to his calls that they will never feel or hear him again. It's a terrifying prospect, but it keeps returning to a simple question of choice. God is love and he created the universe in love. He created you and me in love and true love demands that the other person have a choice to either accept or reject the advances of the one who loves them. Whether we admit it or not, we all know that this is true. For instance, I fell in love with my wife a year before we married. I pursued her and she finally decided that I was a good catch. We have been happily married for a number of years now, but only because she *decided* that I was a good catch. The thing that makes us "happily" married is the knowledge that although I am not nearly the good catch that she thought I was and although there are far better looking men out there than me, she chooses to love me. No one paid her to love me, or forced her, or tricked her. No matter what we walk through together, she continually chooses to love me of her own free will. In my heart, I know that she will remain faithful to our marriage and that no matter what, she loves me. She knows the same thing about her husband. No one paid, forced, or tricked me into marrying her either. My love for her is eternal and she rests easy in the knowledge that her husband is faithful to her. No matter what happens, I will love her unconditionally of my own free will. This level of security is priceless and, because each of us knows that it has been so freely offered by the other, we **choose** not to do anything that would be hurtful to the other or chance losing this treasure that we have. But if I had chosen to ignore her those years ago, she would be gone from me forever by now. But I didn't *ignore* her and she did *decide* to respond to me. The simple answer is that free will must triumph over coercion if it's truly to be love. I would be miserable today if I discovered that my wife had been paid to stay with me, but actually despised me. I would not stand for it. I would set her free in an instant. Or if I discovered that she was being forced to stay with me and tell me that she loves me. I don't want a slave or some kind of obedient pet. I want a wife who, all by herself decided to respond to the love that I was holding out to her. Someone who wants to be with me simply because they want to be with me. Anything less would simply not do.

This is the way that love will work or not work between you and your heavenly Father. You will **decide** whether or not to respond to the love that he is offering you. If you would but turn your heart for a moment in his direction and respond to his love with a little humility, your days of wondering about his voice would be over. He would meet you right there and you would clearly hear the one who has loved you from before the beginning of time. But that terrible choice is now and forever has been ours. His choice was made perfectly clear when he sent his own Son Jesus to die on a Roman cross for our crimes against him. He did this to make sure that there would be absolutely nothing standing between him and you, except for your choice. We all remember that verse in the Bible that we memorized as children. John 3:16: "For God so loved the world, he gave his one and only Son, so that who ever believed in him would not perish but would instead have eternal life." In this one verse we can clearly see the Creator of the whole universe doing everything imaginable to get us to freely respond to his love. He so desperately desires for us to want to return to Him. Please remember that it was in fact we who had abandoned him and not the other way around. And it has been him all along who has been pursuing us, even at his own great cost and not the other way around. But it is also very clear in this verse that the choice is yours. "…that whoever believes." He will not force you, or pay you, or trick you. He will simply continue to love you with a deep abiding love. If you choose to respond to that great love, you will also be one of the happiest people alive. But if you refuse to see the one who created the universe and respond to his love, he will not force you. And at the end of your life, you will have decided your place in eternity, <u>not him</u>. That is why I referred to it as a terrible choice. I know that we all remembered John 3:16, but do you remember what was said in the very next verse--John 3:17? "God did not send his Son into the world to condemn it, but rather he sent him to save it." Isn't that great? God is not mad at us. He is just longing for his children who have wandered away from him, to respond to his great love and to return and live with him forever. But he will never force you to come there or bring you there despite yourself. It truly is your choice as to where you will live forever after this life. He further articulates the wrong choice just two verses later (John 3:19) "This then is the verdict, light has come into the world and men have loved the darkness instead of the light..." Choice! Please don't choose to live eternally apart from him. That awful place was not created for you. It was prepared for Satan and his demons. Yet so many people have chosen that place over heaven. Please choose life.

It is also the reason that you find so many people who have accepted his great gift, crying out to the ones who have not. I know that some of God's children have said some fairly stupid things, but the rest, even at the risk of sounding foolish or being utterly rejected by their peers, continually beg for those who are still refusing his love to humble their hearts and be reconciled to God. They all remember very well what it was like to refuse him and grow increasingly deaf to his calls. And they can also tell you the very moment that they decided to humble their hearts and respond to him. Doesn't it stand to reason that they really may know something now? God said in his word "The fool has said in his heart that there is no God." Believe me, if you are reading these words and have still not responded to God's great love, you can rest assured that he is speaking to you right now through the sloppy writing of one of his happy children. Please don't be a fool. Take the gift. The last thing that I will say about this is that we should solemnly remember that God is not going to die some day and come down and answer to you or me. On the contrary, it is you and I whose time will one day expire here on the earth and it will be you and I who will return to our Maker and answer to him. No matter what you believe, you better be right. Please don't find yourself standing there with life and choices behind you and the option of his gift of eternal life no longer on the table. Choose love. Choose life. Choose now.

CHAPTER TEN

IT'S TIME TO BECOME A MAN

ANY CHALLENGE THAT PRESENTED ITSELF to me from that point on was, in my mind, just another part of the healing process. Although the deficits were many and the approaching road would prove to be a rather long one, I was consoled in the knowledge that the balance of my journey would be traveled in the warm company of the truest of all Fathers. In other words, it no longer mattered where I was going; I knew that I was safe.

This was decidedly the Genesis of my adult life and a multitude of hard lessons which should have been learned in my youth now lay directly before me. Love, marriage, parenting, money management and life planning were all delicate matters about which I hadn't a clue. Each of these in turn and usually at a most inconvenient and vulnerable moment, would introduce themselves to me in the not so distant future. I was young and ever hopeful that God would work his magic quickly and painlessly. He knew how much I hated change. Surely he would understand and make certain accommodations. The plain truth was, had I been left to my own devises; I would have told you that I was very content in my present state, thank you very much. But I was the child and he was the Father and he wasn't asking. Although he absolutely loved me just as I was, he apparently loved me too much to just leave me there, so whether I was ready or not, it was time to become a man.

My usual knee-jerk reaction to such an unwelcomed intrusion would have been a childish outburst of temper, followed by unbelievable pride and pouting. I would then exercise my special gift of self pity, which always came with a hardy side dish of staying mad. I was particularly gifted at staying mad and if I really put forth the effort I could make it last for months. If you wanted evidence of these ridiculous tantrums, you needed only come to my house and observe the numerous holes which decorated every interior door of my home throughout the 1990s; holes which were, strangely enough, about the size of a young man's fist. All of my childhood (which I had been unable to control), along with my final sickening realization that I would actually have very little control of anything in this life, were already of themselves severe cracks in the dam that was holding back an ocean of rage. God deciding to fix his dear little broken child whether he liked it or not would be the glorious blow which fell the great structure. Suddenly all of that deeply held anger was blasting downstream like some emotional tsunami. God just stood there in the torrent and laughed hysterically at his handy work. He obviously didn't like my little dam very much. As the bricks fell and the anger gushed for all to see, I could just sense a big grin of satisfaction on his face. He knew that it was all exposed and out in the daylight now and that was just where he liked that kind of stuff. We would have no choice now but to roll up our sleeves and address it if I intended to be well. In truth, it was as painful as extracting a bad tooth without the benefit of anesthesia and he knew it, but that dam had to go. He looked on with great pity as I crawled out of the rubble and, in his great love; he called a time out so that I could catch my breath. It didn't mean that the issue went away. It simply meant that everyone now knew it was there and we would be dealing with it a little later. But not now, for just then, I was granted what seemed to be the equivalent of a four year sabbatical from all of this fixing; and, boy, did I need it.

I joined my mom's church and dove into the fellowship of those believers with both feet. I sought out every opportunity to be with them. My soul found such refreshment there that I could not stay away. Between my personal fellowship with God and my very outward fellowship with his people, my spirit was soaring higher than ever before. I met with many of them every morning during the week for an hour of prayer before going to work. On Sundays, I volunteered to help out in the Sunday children's ministry and I eagerly attended every mid-week service. Soon, I was invited to assist in the Thursday evening homeless outreach in the downtown area, where we fed, clothed and taught the Bible to the homeless in our town. This was an amazing answer to a specific prayer that I had just been praying. You know, when you're single and only twenty years old you've got loads of free time. So I had just asked the Lord to show me how I could do even more for him. The next night, I received a direct answer. I was approached by a very dear man named Amor Stephen. He was in charge of that ministry and he asked me to consider joining them the following night. I had never done anything like that before and, although I felt a bit apprehensive about the whole thing, I graciously accepted his invitation. I met him and his small team of volunteers at the church the next night. We loaded up into a van and drove downtown. Once there, I did not wander far from the team. The homeless men and women were very familiar with the ministry and knew where to be on Thursday evenings if they wanted a change of clothes or something to eat. Once those needs were met, we simply sat around, sang some songs and chatted with them about more eternal matters. I will never forget that first night out as long as I live. I was sitting there on some old dilapidated brick wall listening to Amor talk to this relatively young homeless guy, who he had obviously been talking to on previous Thursdays. He was simply letting the guy know that God loved him, but the guy just seemed so depressed. And then it just happened. As I sat there listening to their conversation, I was also aimlessly flipping pages in my Bible. I was not looking for anything in particular; I was just flipping some pages. By chance, I flipped it open to the New Testament letter from Paul to the Philippians. It fell open at chapter one and as I glanced down at it, my eyes fell to verse six. The verse reads *"I am confident of this, that He who began a good work in you will carry it on to completion until the day of Christ Jesus."* As I looked up from reading it, I noticed that they had stopped talking and were now looking directly at me. I mean right at me, as if they were waiting for an answer to some question that they had just asked and that I had somehow missed. Then Amor said to me "Jim, do you have anything that you want to share with this man?" The nervous half of me wanted to say "No, you're doing fine, sir." But I didn't. Instead I followed my heart and said "Uh, well, I did just see this nice verse here that might encourage him." They courteously adjusted their seating position to face me and waited. As I nervously read the passage, I was stunned as both men began to cry. I stopped abruptly and said "What did I do?" They smiled through their tears. Amor looked at the guy and said "I didn't say anything to him." Then Amor said to me "You didn't know this, but just last week as we were sitting right here talking, the Lord gave me the exact same passage to share with this young man. It seems that God is talking to him." I could not believe what I had just heard. I felt like shouting out loud so that everyone in the city could hear me "God just used me! Did anyone just see that?" But I kept quiet and allowed them to enjoy the moment. Then we all had tears in our eyes.

Well, I was hooked. I was there every Thursday after that. Each week it was the same routine; clothes, food, songs and some conversation. There could often be as many as ten to twenty homeless folks there with us and they particularly enjoyed Amor's banjo and singing. He had begun teaching me to play the guitar and soon I was joining him in the music as he led the singing. One night as we drove back to the church, I said to Amor "I think that we really should consider bringing a small sound system and a pulpit with us next week and conduct a regular service." His response was swift, as though he had been anticipating such a suggestion. He looked at me and said "I agree--and you will be doing the preaching." I said "What? I think that I am not alone when I say that you have completely taken leave of your senses on that one, brother." I fully expected to hear the rest of the team thunderously agreeing with me and snapping this guy back to reality. But the van grew strangely quiet. Then one of the older women in the back of the van spoke up and said "Amor is right, Jim." Amor didn't miss a beat and, with the biggest grin on his face, he said "Be ready next Thursday." What did I just get myself into? I meant that he should preach, not me. I wasn't ready for this.

The next day, I opened my Bible and began to pray for help. "Oh, God," I prayed, "What in the world am I going to say to these people?" In a flash, my mind was awash with things that I wanted to say. I could barely contain my excitement and suddenly I could not wait until Thursday. I was twenty years old the night that I preached my first sermon. The title of that first message was "Why does God seem so far away?" Amor taped my sermons each week as a gift to me and I kept them all. I listened to them many years later and realized that my first brilliant sermon was only the first in a long line of seriously lame sermons. I have no idea why anyone sat there and listened to me. If I were sitting there, I would have left. But now I deeply treasure them, along with the time that I spent there with Amor and the team. I was now the one doing the preaching every Thursday and soon I became known as "the young man preacher" by my homeless congregation. Life had never been so good. I could have literally stayed right there for the remainder of my days.

After two years of this fervor, I was approached in the autumn of 1988 by the pastor and the leadership of the church. They, having witnessed my dedication and development, presented me with the very real prospect that I was actually called to this work as a full time minister. They suggested setting aside two years for studying at a small, private school, where I could prepare for such a calling. I was elated. To me, this was the Lord Jesus himself placing his stamp of approval on me. Many members of our congregation, who all deeply loved me and who agreed with their assessment, each pitched in some money for my travel expenses. Within a few weeks, I was on my way to Bible school.

It was a thrilling time as changes to my life were now coming at me in rapid fire succession. It was the kind of excitement that makes you grit your teeth and nearly lose your breath. As I left town, my young mind was filling up with lofty ideas. Chief among those early dreams was that of finishing school and returning as a hero to my loving church, who would then offer me a full- time position on the ministry staff. Oh, yeah, baby, I had it all figured out. Those two years at that small Bible school were definitely two of the best years of my life. I never missed a day of class, unless it was with the dean's blessing so that I could go preach somewhere.

All of this intense following after God was having a profoundly positive effect on my relationship with my brother Eli as well. We had all but become estranged from one another over the past number of years. But after some heartfelt repentance on both of our parts during my summer break at home, he decided not only to join the church, but to also join me at the Bible school during my second year. And although he had his own difficult journey ahead, it was great to have him there with me.

Shortly after our arrival back at the school in the autumn of 1989, we received word that Grandma Wischer had suddenly and unexpectedly passed away. It had been a few years since my last visit and the news knocked me back on my heels. The last time that we were together we had talked about Grandpa's conversion just prior to his passing and how it had convinced her that it was time that she too responded to God's great love. Once again, through the tears, I was comforted in the knowledge that they were both at home in Heaven waiting for my arrival. Eli and I took a few days off from our school work to drive up to Florence to be at the funeral. It was a nice reunion despite the sad circumstances. We got to spend some time with certain family that we had not seen in a while. It was also at this gathering that I witnessed the full measure of enmity which existed between my dad and his three siblings. Although I had previously heard about it from dad years earlier, I had simply brushed it aside as more of his exaggerated conjecture. But hearing it from the other side of the equation was truly depressing. They sat me down at Grandma's dining room table and began to explain that they were not going to allow dad to come to the funeral. I said "Are you nuts? Do you really think that he is not going to come? It's his mother, for crying out loud." I was truly astonished at the level of animosity that was pouring out of them like a well-rehearsed song. All three of them in turn justified their bitterness to me over the span of an hour before I had simply had enough. I walked away from that meeting, leaving them with a request that they make no attempt at inviting me to choose a side. Dad received the same request from me years earlier, but neither he nor his brothers and sister could resist the temptation of filling my ears with their resentment. This is probably the reason that I find it nearly impossible to spend time with any of them to this day. I don't hate them. On the contrary, I loved them all very much and still do. I was just disappointed and really didn't want to listen to it anymore. I had enough baggage of my own and wasn't at all interested in carting any of theirs around.

Before completely drifting away from dad and after leaving that ridiculous meeting, I felt a new fierce determination to rescue what was left of our relationship if I could. He and Paula had, of course, defied the wishes of the others and drove up from Florida to say goodbye to Grandma. While they were there, I made it a point to go to them and make amends. We all said sorry and hugged and determined to start afresh. They seemed genuinely interested in this new refreshing upbeat attitude of mine, so I spent the rest of the evening recounting for them my recent walk through the rich garden of faith. They listened intently and although not in full agreement with all that I believed, they were proud of my newly found happiness. It was a great evening of reconciliation and we eventually parted ways with a promise that we would meet again for Christmas at their home. Two months later, we reunited at their home in Florida for the traditional family bake night and it was truly a great Christmas.

Dad and Paula then drove up the following summer to join my mother and attend our graduation from Bible school. It was a grand gesture which solidified our newly healed relationship so much more. It was now becoming easier to find reasons to spend time together and over the next eight years I never missed a family bake night.

As it turned out, I was going to need as much family time as I could get my hands on, because those next eight years were also going to be filled with some really personal faith-shaking disappointments. Oh, I know there's nothing new about disappointments. There's not even anything new about the extraordinary way that they tend to shape a young man's faith in the end. But I didn't know any of that back then. In fact, just like anyone else, I would have argued that I didn't need any further shaping and that I was fine. But, of course, I was not fine at all.

That said, it seemed that the season of fixing had returned and my quiet little respite was obviously drawing to its conclusion. I guess God must have thought that I had sufficiently caught my breath, because once again I found myself in the crosshairs of some very hard medicine indeed. I did not agree with God's assessment of my readiness and as a matter of fact, I was really quite hoping that he might have just forgotten all about that stuff. But, nope, him didn't forget.

I think that we all may have to admit at some point that disappointments are probably one of God's best tools for growing us up. But we'll never admit it while we are going through it, will we? The problem with disappointment is in the way that it usually just arrives unannounced. It just shows up and muscles its way into our quiet little lives at any time, convenient or not. Then, ready or not, it's on. We muster a defensive front in the interest of preserving control of our own lives, but God has seen that trick a million times. He just brings it. Then we resort back to being four year olds again. We kick and scream and offer God a few wags of our fists and some unsolicited opinions about his handling of things. If we're at all typical, we will probably throw in a few colorful metaphors that we later regret. Oh, yeah, you know what I'm talking about. But once all of that painful work has finished and we find ourselves standing in the surreal quiet of their aftermath, we can't help but admit that we have in fact grown and that, like them or not, disappointment has actually accomplished its intended good.

As I mentioned earlier, I returned to Florida after graduation with ambitions of joining the ministry staff at our church. Imagine my surprise when I learned that I had not only been denied that position, but was instead about to be hurled alive into a burning crucible of reality and hardship. Not just any old furnace either. Oh, no, sir-ee. This one had been stoked just for me. It was dark and ugly and appeared to have been specifically designed with a special feature that would relentlessly burn and chip away at my well-groomed fakeness. Oh, yes and it was definitely hot enough to continue burning until it had literally unmasked the real me. This crucible was fierce, maybe even cruel and unusual. It was hard and mean and unfair. This thing even had a name. They called it "*Manuel Labor*". AAHHH!!! You've got to be kidding me! I didn't know it then, but the church elders had not been entertaining the same ambitions for my employment that I had been. The position was given to another guy--a good guy, so I was happy for him, but it was impossible to hide the disappointment that hit me in the stomach like a truck. I was doing a pretty good job, at first, of keeping a lid on my frustration, but then reality hit. I was twenty four years old and I needed a job. I couldn't just mooch off of my mom forever. So I lifted my eyes toward the stars and again asked my Heavenly Father for help. Almost before the words left my lips, his answer came. The following Sunday I was approached by a man from our church and was offered a job with his construction company. YEA! CONSTRUCTION! Again, are you kidding me? This was not at all what I meant when I was praying. I didn't want to be a total fool and just reject an offered income, but God! Construction? Really? I longed for a secondary and far less strenuous offer, but it never came. There seemed to be no out for me, so Monday morning I strapped on my boots and was on the jobsite before the sun even came up. Have you ever felt like life was just happening to you and there was nothing you could do about it? Well, that was me right then and the whole thing was quietly slipping from my control faster than I could contain it.

It only took a few days out in the blazing Florida sun to melt away what remained of my concealing smile and, oh yeah, it was definitely on. Now that the façade was out of the way, the angry little man on the inside was free to show the world his true colors. In my mind, it was definitely a temporary arrangement. There was no way that God would have spent so much time preparing me for ministry, then simply send me out to pour concrete for some guy who obviously had no interest in my true potential. I wasted little time informing my new boss that I would be gone just as soon as God opened an available and more appropriate ministry door for me. Which, I added, would probable be in a matter of weeks, not months. I then returned to my work and began singing loud enough for everyone to hear, while he just stood there shaking his head. Yeah, I was that guy too. Can't you just in-vision that whole silly scene? What a putts I was. Anyway, he just laughed at me and said "We'll see if you're still singing two years from now." I quickly reminded him that I would already be a distant memory for him in two years, since I would very likely be gone in a few weeks. He smiled arrogantly and I decided that I hated him. Unfortunately for me, I would have to work with him every day until God rescued me and swept me away to my "higher calling". I knew it was coming; I just had to hang on for a week or two.

Well, the weeks quickly turned into months and I found myself hating this guy more than ever. I told you my true colors were coming out. There I was, God's little minister, standing there hating the man who had given me a job. "What is God doing here?" quickly began to turn into "Who does God think he is?" The stew was now reaching its intended boiling point. God knew exactly what he was doing. The potter was cooking his little pot to remove its impurities and his little pot was screaming and cussing him out the whole way. But to his credit and in his true form, he never got mad at me for it. He would just stand next to me, stroking my head and reassuring me. "It's okay, little pot. I know it hurts, but I'm here with you and I'll never leave you. It won't last much longer. Be brave, little pot."

My boss's name was Verle Conrad and there was no doubt that he was a true blue construction type, just like his father before him. Now before I make myself sound like a total jerk, we did eventually become friends. He surprised me one day at work when he broke down and revealed to me the reason for his gruff attitude about my wanting to leave. I have never forgotten his words to me and, although they failed to impress me at that time, there were never truer words spoken. He said "I just can't stand seeing you young guys blow in here, singing and praising the Lord like that until the work gets hard. Then you disappear. Sure, you learned the Bible; so did I. I also went to Bible College for a couple of years." I said "Then you of all people should understand what I am feeling." He said "Yeah, I do. But what you're going to have to learn is that although you studied the Bible in the class room, you're only going to learn how to be a man of God out here. These are the fires that will build integrity and character if you let them and believe me; God's not going to let you leave here until you stop hating it." I walked away from him mumbling something clever like "Sure, buddy, don't hold your breath." Well, I'm glad that he didn't hold his breath, because seven years later I was still there, working as one of his foremen. Unbelievable! We eventually became friends and I realized that he had been right all along. During those years of sweat, toil and putting up with other vile constructions types, God had literally exposed and began removing the rage that was in me. Some may argue that given what I had lived through, I had the right to be enraged. As debatable as that may be, I was the one who had to admit that the rage wasn't hurting anyone but me. Besides, the job did have its benefits as well. By the time I was twenty eight years old, my strapping, bronze body and snow white hair were turning more than a few heads and as fleeting as it was, it did help me to feel a little better through that string of disappointments. I was also reminded of that little prayer that I had prayed my first day back to church a few years ago. "Anywhere you want me to go, Lord, any thing you want me to do, you have the rest of my life if you want it". He obviously wanted it and, believe it or not, with his help I even stopped hating my place in the world.

While I was busy building my physique on the construction site, a third and far more powerful rumble of disappointment began to bite at me. This one was about to touch the very deepest part of me and would even shake my very soul. I was a very young and immature Christian before I left for Bible school and, as you can imagine, my level of naivety back then was off the charts. You know the type, easy fodder for the unbelieving intellectual or some kind of practice toy for the visiting Jehovah's Witnesses. In the beginning, I simply believed what those church leaders were teaching me and felt brilliant as I learned to embrace and even teach others the same. Like a baby bird with eyes closed and mouth wide open, I ate what ever they dropped in and, in no time, I was fat with bad doctrine. This blind faith in my leaders went on for years until a firm belief system had been well established in me and was doing its damage. This particular disappointment had its beginning during those next couple of years at Bible school. Once there and away from the ever watchful influence of our church leaders, I was able to make a very healthy change in the way I took in information. This was a good thing, as I was literally growing sick of the same old meat and potatoes self-centered gospel bunk that I had been receiving for so long now. I determined from that point on to let the Bible stand alone and speak for itself. This meant that no matter which professor stood before us, I was resolved to now, as it were, eat the hay and spit out the sticks. It doesn't take a genius to tell if someone is messing with the text and I was no longer going to stand for it. I wanted to know God and his word and nothing else. It also helped that I was actually reading the thing for myself in those days. Oh, yes, I was! And how I bathed in its salvation and how I breathed in the sweet smell of sound doctrine. I stuck around because there were actually a few great teachers there who kept my faith in God growing in the right direction. But in doing so, I had inadvertently discovered the very disturbing truth about the shear numbers of bad teachers that were actually out there. I began to see with remarkable clarity the two camps and with it came the beginning of a great heartache. There were, of course, the ones who actually knew the Bible and taught it like it was written. Then there were the ones who didn't have a clue what was truly there, but were making a good living off making us believe that they did. I am afraid that the latter have driven a great number away from God. Anyway, the more I read, the more unsettled I became in what I had believed all this time. Little by little the word of God was picking away at all of that rubbish that I had been taught back at my church. As hard as it was to do, I was finally forced to realize that the guy who was in charge of our church simply couldn't have read the Bible for himself. The stuff that he was teaching, as nice as it sounded, was simply not at all biblical. Of course you couldn't tell him that--in fact no one could ever tell him anything, which was in and of itself a huge problem. This is, in my opinion, one of the principle failures of that branch of Christianity to this day. Its leader's staunch refusal in submitting to any form of accountability leaves its parishioners constantly vulnerable to their shallow heretical non-sense. You see the problem with this ridiculous health and wealth gospel, which I had just spent six years of my own life in, is its intoxicating message of self indulgence. The whole thing is usually propagated by some local charismatic type "A" control freak, who simply refuses to be accountable to anyone. No matter what town I have ever lived in or visited, I have observed a thriving health and wealth church operating there. The reason for the numbers is no mystery either. The message is awesomely seductive. With the proper amount of faith, you can get God to give you life on *your* own terms. You can literally, as some have asserted, write your own ticket. But without this "proper amount" of faith, you get nothing from him and are in fact in danger of the very flames of hell. You are instantly thrown into an impossible grind of trying to make or keep God happy with your performance. This message is pure heresy. The wealth never comes and, after having been told hundreds of times that the problem is in fact their own faith (or the lack thereof), the parishioner begins to become extremely disillusioned. This inevitably makes them resentful toward a God to whom, no matter how much sweat they offer, refuses to be pleased with their effort. Eventually most of those who have been burned for a while make their exit and walk right past the next crowd of eager listeners who are on their way in. Some leave never to darken the door of a church again, while others who have simply read the Bible for themselves during their frustrating stay, find a new and refreshing congregation to meet with where the Bible is actually taught. In either case, the jokers who run these health and wealth shows have no shortage of fresh new faces that seem all too eager to check their intellect at the door and part with their money. I'm not mocking them. I was one of them and was well on my way to becoming one of their leaders. But it is what it is. This is all easy to type about now, but back then it was a much larger blow than missing out on some coveted ministry position. All of the things that I had earnestly believed for half a dozen years was essentially being erased right before my eyes and I found myself feeling a bit lost again. When it was finally all gone and there was literally nothing left of my faith except for its foundation, which was Jesus Himself, I just stood there shivering like a wet naked dog. This was always the goal and even though it was the very spot that he had intended this disappointment to bring me to, he had no intention of leaving me there. For, with one touch of the Savior's warm hand, the rebuilding began. In 1991, I made my way out of that awful rat race and located a relatively new congregation in my town. These people were actually studying the Bible and not messing around with it. The church was called "Agape Christian Fellowship" and I was hooked from my first visit.

The pastor, forty something year old Carl Dixon, was actually teaching the Bible and had no apparent underlying motive mixed in with the message. I had studied the Bible for a few years now and knew that what I was hearing was the real deal. I immediately joined their happy little fellowship and again dove in with both feet. They had recently begun hosting a second service on Sunday morning to accommodate the growing numbers and there was no shortage of opportunities to plug in if you wanted to. I informed the director of the children's ministry that I was eager to help out in any way I could. He was glad to hear it and asked me if I would consider teaching the junior high Sunday school class during the second service. I joyfully accepted his offer and for about the next ten years you could find me right there teaching each new group of sixth, seventh and eighth graders who passed through. Throughout that same decade, I hosted and taught a weekly adult Bible study in my home as well. I also served as a deacon for a few years and assisted on the mission's board, taking numerous missions trips. There I was afforded the privilege of preaching and teaching the Bible in a number of places around the world. Back at home, I preached to our congregation whenever given the opportunity. I was again feeling very much at home and up to that point, it had actually been the best decade of my life.

It was also during this decade that I met a young arrogant political science graduate who had also recently joined our fellowship. This guy looked like he was on the fast track to a career in politics and even though we were around the same age, I was sure that I wasn't going to like him at all. You know the type--never paying attention when you are speaking to them because they are always too busy looking at their watch or checking out some other conversation across the room. Always too busy networking to stop and be a human for a minute. Yeah, you know the type. He reminded me of a jerk that I knew about a year earlier back at that Word of Faith church that I used to attend. Unfortunately, that jerk was me. I was obviously judging my own faults in him and the funny thing was he never even knew that any of this was going on in my head. I had all but convinced myself that we would never be friends the same way I had written Verle off when I first met him. If this is all sounding a bit familiar, you won't be shocked by any surprise ending here either. This man's name is Tim Polak and for the past fifteen plus years, he's been my best friend. Being at roughly the same place in our spiritual journey when we met, we had far more in common than either of us knew and unbeknownst to either one of us it was going to be the glue that bound us together from that point on. Over the years there has been nothing hidden in our lives that the other didn't know about. We each had our own demons to fight off, but neither of us left the other to fight alone. He was my best man when I got married and I was his. To this day, if I need encouragement, I know that he is just a phone call away. I mention him here because from this point on in my story, he has been there to bear witness to my journey and has been a significant part of my spiritual growth. You will most definitely see him again in later chapters.

CHAPTER ELEVEN

LEARNING TO TRUST GOD

WHILE THE HARD LABOR OF the concrete profession was chipping away at my anger management problem, God must have thought that it was time for me to move on to my next lesson. It was time for me to learn how to truly trust him, no matter what, even if his plans were not the same as mine.

In the summer of 1993, three years into my journey with Verle, he decided to quit early one day and take us all to lunch. I'm sure now that it was utterly the hand of providence that we ended up eating at this particular restaurant, even though it seemed like a random pick. While sitting there waiting for our orders to arrive, I heard the very loud and very distinguishing laugh of a man whom I had not seen for over three years. I could not see his face, but no one else in the world had that laugh. So I got out of my seat to investigate. I turned the corner and saw this laughing man sitting there having lunch with another very good friend of mine, Mr. Jon Franson, who was, as it turned out, a mutual friend of ours. The man with the unique laugh was Israel Airabach. He and his wife were classmates of mine back in Bible school. After graduation, we had all hugged and parted ways, never expecting to see each other again in this life. And to my utter amazement, there he was, seven hundred miles south and three years later, sitting at a table with my friend Jon. Upon seeing me walk up, Israel leapt to his feet, embraced me in a big hug and in that familiar Israeli accent yelled "Brotha Jeem!" Jon stood up also with a big smile on his face, shook my hand and said "Hi, Brother Jimmy. You know Israel?" To which I responded "why yes I do, but how do you know him?" I sat down for a few minutes and listened as Israel explained how he had just met Jon and was inviting him to go with him to the Holy Land to work on a piece of property that his father had just given to him. I was astonished at this spectacle, but before I could utter a word in response, Israel blurted out, "And you should come too, my beloved brotha!" I was finally able to snap out of my trance and responded "Yeah, that sounds like great fun, but since I will probably have trouble paying for this lunch, I will most likely not be purchasing a flight to Israel today." He laughed out loud and again yelled, this time so that the entire restaurant could hear him "Oh Brotha Jeem, with God all things are possible!" I said "Then I will pray and wait for his answer." We shared a few more laughs and again said goodbye. Later that day, as I arrived home from work, I heard my phone ringing. I ran to catch it. I was pleasantly surprised to again hear my friend Jon Franson on the other end. "Hey, Brother Jimmy" he said in his usual cheerful tone. "Hey, Jonny," I replied, "what's happening?" He said "Wasn't that great that Israel invited both of us to the Holy Land?" I said "Yes, it was and I will be thinking and praying about it." To which he replied "I think the time for praying about it is past. I'm buying both of us a ticket, so get ready to travel." I just stood there speechless for a minute. Excitement began to well up at a feverish pace as my mind darted back and forth, trying to wrap itself around the meaning of this incredible offer. I had been serving at the Calvary Chapel of Sarasota (the current name for the Agape Christian Fellowship) for a few years and had become good friends with several of our sponsored missionaries. As I grew closer to these missionaries, I could not help but feel a bit of a calling to go and help them or perhaps start my own overseas work. Could this Holy Land invitation be a confirmation of those strong feelings? I ecstatically accepted my friend's generous invitation and began planning my first ever overseas trip. In a side note, this was typical Jon Franson. He is by no means wealthy, materially speaking, but is without a doubt one of the most generous people that I have ever had the privilege to know in this life. He carries a genuine burden to be a help and a blessing to his fellow man, faithfully obeying that high call. I hope at the end of my life here, people can say the same of me.

Verle, who was also a generous man, granted me the vacation time with some pay and a few short weeks later I found myself sitting next to my friend on a 747, preparing for takeoff. Twenty-four hours later we were in Israel, standing on the wall of the old city in Jerusalem, staring down at the city of David. As the cool evening desert wind rushed up the side of that ancient hill and blew my hair back, I literally found it hard to breath. With tears welling, I caught my breath and thought to myself: who gets to do this? This land is particularly meaningful to those who walk with God and there I was standing there as if I were gazing off of my own back porch. It was magnificent, but why was I there? I had really never thought of traveling to the Holy Land and now there I was standing on that wall just drinking it all in. We were going to be there for a few weeks and Israel's apartment was too small for us to share, so we set out to locate a place to live. After checking several places, we literally stumbled across a small Bible college down in Bethlehem, which was appropriately called the Bethlehem Bible College. Israel said that he knew the director and that he would probably get us a room for a small price. We rang the bell and instantly the smiling face of Dr. Bishara Awad appeared at the door. Dr Awad, who was the president and cofounder of the school, seemed so delighted to meet us and welcomed us in. He told us that the college would probably charge us ten dollars a day for a bed and breakfast arrangement. We were thrilled and couldn't believe that for ten bucks a day, we were going to get to live in Bethlehem for a while. With warm smiles all around, Bishara saw us to our room. So began a friendship that has lasted to this day.

Jon and I were a couple of novice travelers who had no tour guide to keep us from getting ourselves into trouble. We were completely ignorant about the geopolitical landscape that we were just trekking around in as though we owned it and were probably, albeit innocently, sending out all the wrong signals to the people who actually lived there. We didn't mean it. We were men and as is usually the case with men, we found ourselves being clumsily dragged around town by our empty bellies. Every man knows that tending to an empty belly always trumps political correctness. Walking around Bethlehem like a couple of seasoned locals was truly one of the highlights of that trip. It was really a memorable experience.

You could never have convinced me then, but this trip was actually going to be the beginning of one of the biggest disappointments of my life. I was too caught up in the awesomeness of the place to have been able to see anything difficult coming at me just then, but it was coming alright. I was just so caught up. This was the land of God. It was the place to where God had called Abraham. It was where the kings and prophets had come and gone. It was where Jesus himself had lived, died and risen again and where the apostles had first preached the message. Everything that I am and that I believe is that land and there I was mixing it up with the locals as if I had always lived there. Wow!

Early each morning, Israel would drive to the college from Jerusalem to pick us up in his tiny little car and off we would go, out to the property that his father had given to him. It was an exquisite yet hotly contested little piece of land that he now owned. The plot was situated on the side of Prophet Samuel's mountain, a few miles outside of Jerusalem. The property has a couple of natural caves on it with fresh water springs bubbling up from deep within. These form crystal clear, ice cold pools which are several feet deep. Some of the local Orthodox Jews coveted the property because of its religious connection with the prophet Samuel. Several would come almost daily to dip themselves sanctimoniously into the cold waters of its sacred caves. A local Bedouin needed the land and its caves to graze and water his goats. He also made a daily appearance with his herd to poach a refreshing drink or two. And, finally, there was the nearby Arab village who simply claimed it as theirs, because they did not want to see that land fall into the hands of the Israeli government, who would most assuredly build a new Jewish settlement. All of this bickering in the face of my friend's legitimate title deed was a real cultural shock for me. Was there no law? Was there no 911 to call? Back home this would have been sorted out in ten seconds. You either own the land or you don't. It's not rocket science. It really was a strange reality to witness, but I guess these land disputes are quite common in that country.

We would work hard all day with our friend and then both Israel and his wife would often take us sightseeing in the evening. Sometimes we would just return to the college and spend the evenings sitting on the roof and looking out over Bethlehem. That never got old either. Sitting up there and staring wide eyed at the surrounding villages during those cool aired evenings is a beautiful sight that has drawn me back many times now. Our time in that ancient place was truly indescribable, but still I found myself wondering why I was really there. What a stooge. Why couldn't I just shut up and enjoy the moment? Why did it have to be so mystical? I kept thinking that all we were really doing was helping Israel build a wall on his land and taking some nice pictures, but then it happened. I finally found the trouble that I had been so desperately seeking.

A few days prior to my departure, Bishara came to our room to extend an invitation for us to join him as his guest at a concert later that evening.

It seemed that the college sponsored a choir which traveled around the world as sort of an ambassador for the school. They were apparently quite good and it was our good luck that we were in Bethlehem at the same time they were. Jon was too exhausted to attend, but at age twenty-seven, I was never too tired to go out at night. So I got myself ready, tossed a couple of "old man" jokes at Jon on my way out and walked next door. Bishara met me at the door, offered me some refreshments and began introducing me to some supposedly important people who had also come to hear the choir. I had no idea who these people were, but the introductions made me feel important as well. Bishara had been that kind of a gracious host during our entire stay. A few minutes later, we took our seats and the choir took the stage. It took only ten seconds for me to spot her; first row, third from the left. She was beautiful.

Now before I go any further, let me just make a few clarifications. First of all, is there anything so ridiculously devastating as a boy falling in love? I assure you the answer is a resounding no. It really is pathetic to watch isn't it? It's all so wonderful and so awful at the same time, as any young man can attest. I am saying this because I don't want anyone to read more into this next part than is really here. What was happening to me at that moment had already happened to me many times prior to ever seeing this girl and it would happen to me many more times after she was gone. It's just the way it goes for boys I guess. If we're lucky, one of these beautiful creatures will decide to keep us and love us forever, but until then we are doomed to ride this same wave of unbearable misery that we call romance. One cruel fiction after another will toy with us and crush us, before God's mercy helps us forget. Then we await the next. Or should I say we go looking for the next. Well, it's a vicious plight and apparently I had just stumbled into my next, and there she was.

As I stood there staring at her, I momentarily came to my senses and reminded myself that I was flying home in a few days and that it would be extremely problematic and even stupid to allow myself to fall in love at this juncture. Unfortunately that little bit of self-administered advice would prove to be the last of the common sense. I couldn't help it. It was too late. I was already in over my head.

Bishara told me her name and informed me that she would be at the young adult's Bible study down at the Baraka Church the following day. He told me that the church was only a few blocks from the college and he was certain that she would be happy to meet me as well. I told him that I would go.

The next day I made my way to the church, dragging my feet just a little and wondered just what I would say to this girl. Maybe it was that warm dusty air or the grand thoughts of what may lie ahead. But my pace was slow and my thoughts were quite high. What was I supposed to say to her? What did I think I was doing? What was I thinking? And therein lies the oldest wrinkle in the history of wrinkles, I wasn't.

I must have arrived too early, because no one was there yet. The small driveway wound down a gentle hill and deposited me at the door of a very old building indeed. The stone masonry was as tan as every other building in town, but seemed to be quite a bit older than most. It was a quaint little structure which overlooked a large valley. On the opposite side of the valley the land re-ascended into the hillside village of Beit-Jala. The two seemed to have been setting there looking at each other forever. The church building itself was small, but it suited the needs of this small congregation.

I sat on a large rock bolder that was protruding out of the ground and stared quietly for a while. I wondered just how long this ancient stone had been there and who else in history may have sat on it. The Holy Land has that effect on everyone. Your mind can't help but drift into antiquity and wonder. I sat there on that old rock for a while and stared and thought about my upcoming meeting. As I drifted farther and farther away from the safe port of reality, a warm anesthetizing cloud of desire settled in over me. I had officially taken leave of my senses. Do you see what I mean about romance? It's just so pitiful.

As far as I was now concerned, it was God himself who had orchestrated this entire journey to finally reveal his plan for my wife; I mean my life. Who could have imagined me in the Holy Land as a missionary, married to a lovely young girl? It all seemed so wonderfully clear. There was no reaching or saving me now; I was completely convinced. Emotions of that magnitude, coupled with an intoxicating sense that this thing had in fact been delivered to me from God's own hand, were a real recipe for true disappointment. And although I did not know it, I was about to walk through the darkest valley of disappointment that I had ever encountered in my adult life.

Now as a courtesy to this young lady, Bishara had informed her of my plan to meet her, so she knew that I was going to be there and thus avoided an embarrassing ambush. But what would I say to her? Should I just blurt out "I'm in love with you?" That never worked in the past. What would I say after that? I literally had no idea who she was or what she believed or where she was headed in this life. Unfortunately, the imperative in discovering the answers to these important questions had already been abandoned hours ago. I was now fully floating in the blind realm of infatuation and completely believed that it was God's plan to thrill me with her love.

Just then, a young teenage boy named Gabriel Hanna entered through the main gate of the church yard. He seemed delighted to meet me and, after some small talk, challenged me to a game of basketball. This was a nice distraction from all of the noise in my mind and it gave my heart a more legitimate reason for beating as fast as it was. Little by little, around a dozen young "twenty somethings" arrived for the Bible study. This was my first real encounter with Palestinian believers, other than Bishara and it was a real treat to meet them. Soon, the study began and there was no sign of the girl. I was sure that she was letting me know that she was not interested and I was crushed. After the meeting, I said goodbye to my new friends and slowly walked back to the college. Bishara met me when I got back. I got the feeling that he had been pacing around like a worried parent, wondering how our meeting would go. When I told him what had happened, he raced to his phone and called her family. After an agonizingly short Arabic conversation, he hung up and informed me that she in fact wanted to meet me, but had gotten sick after the concert last night and could not make it to the Bible study. But, he added, she will be at the Bethlehem University tomorrow to register for her next school year and would like to meet me there. Well, that was obviously great to hear. With a deep sigh of relief, my countenance once again lifted itself from the pit of utter rejection and dared to cast its gaze upwards once again towards the lofty peaks of love. Things were looking up again and I would just have to lose one more night of sleep.

That next sleepless night gave me time to calm my fragile nerves by systematically justifying what I was feeling. I had just met some very wonderful and fascinating Palestinian brothers and sisters who may prove eager to extend their hand of fellowship to me. Now it all really seemed to be coming together. The "chance meeting" with Israel in that restaurant, Jon buying me a ticket, meeting Bishara and these other believers and finally falling for a beautiful girl could only mean one thing. It no longer mattered what God actually thought about all of this. I was now at the wheel and I was on a roll. It is truly amazing how we all do that. You talk about turning a mole hill into a mountain. God may be simply walking along with us one day, just minding his own business. Then, just in passing, he whispers some small thing to us like "Hey, look at that beautiful mountain over there." We could just act like an adult in that situation and say something back to him like "Yes, Lord that is a lovely piece of your handiwork," but not us. Oh, no, sir-ee. Instantly, our restless minds take over and add "Yes, Lord, I see it and you must want me to climb it for your glory!" But before He can say "No, I just wanted you to see it," we are already halfway up the thing and getting ourselves into all kinds of trouble. Later, after we have thoroughly beaten ourselves up and discovered that the climb was not such a good idea, we sink into disappointment and blame him for not stopping us. Sound familiar?

The following day I made my way to the university to meet her. After she took care of some important school business and gave me the nickel tour we finally sat down to talk for a while. I put on the most charming face that I could and explained to her what had happened to me and what I was feeling. She told me that she really didn't know what to think, but said that she was enjoying my company and would like very much to walk with me back to the Bible College. So we did just that. Once at the college, I could feel our time slipping away like water through my hand and I could do nothing to prevent its escape. Amazingly, just two days prior I was feeling eager anticipation of my flight home, where everything would be normal again. Now, no matter how hard I wished, I could do nothing to expand the minutes. I knew that she couldn't just stay there with me forever and would have to be getting home soon. But I also knew that this would be it. This was the time to make that all important first impression. After we had talked for a while and she had finally had a little more time to think through what I was saying to her. She wisely informed me that it was probably not a good idea for us to attempt a relationship of that nature. She felt that it would be riddled with difficulties. She was already well on her way to a great education and career. She was also very happy right where she was and had no intentions of leaving her family, friends, or the life that she knew. She was also smart enough to know that even though I was convinced that I would be living there in her town as a missionary; that may well prove not to be the case. She was thinking much more clearly than I was. I tried to convince her otherwise, but she could see right through that cloud that I was lost in and she stood her ground.

We concluded our meeting with the promise that we could maintain our new friendship and that we could wait and see what may happen. For her that meant exactly that, with a strong leaning toward a probable decline of the offer. But for an extremely love sick boy, that was as good as a yes and just enough to keep hope alive. Those futile hopes would string me along for three more years before finally releasing me back to my senses. She was never mean or cruel to me, it's just that we were both young and we simply did not know how to just let go in a situation like that. If she had been a little older and wiser, she probably would have simply put me out of my misery during our first meeting, as so many other girls had done in the past. If I had been a bit older and wiser, I probably wouldn't have put her in such an awkward position in the first place.

Jon had decided to remain in Israel for a few more weeks, but I had to get back to work, so the plane trip home was lonely and quiet. Unfortunately, my fogged-in brain had many long hours of idleness to continue working on this fantasy. I was preparing the good report that I would deliver to my church once I got home. Oh, how thrilled they would be upon hearing all that "God" had done for me. God really must have been rubbing his head just then. I mean really! He was just trying to show me a beautiful mountain to look at, but it was too late. I was already halfway up the thing. I know that He must have called out to me. But I was too busy climbing to hear Him.

My church did eagerly welcome me home and listened in astonishment to my story. With the powerful "God spin" that I put on the testimony; they couldn't help but agree that God was obviously calling me to work in the Holy Land. Now in fairness to me, I would have happily served the Lord in that place, but I had already become less interested in the work and far more interested in getting the girl. Oh, yeah, I was definitely ready to be a missionary: NOT! But who could tell this headstrong young man such a thing? Not even God was getting through to me. I'm just keeping it real here, people; I'm just keeping it real.

I returned to my job the following day with a new song in my heart and this time Verle felt less tempted to crush the singing. He genuinely felt happy for me. When I was not at work, I was off at some missions' conferences preparing for life as a missionary. I traveled all over the eastern United

States looking for the right missions' agency to join, while simultaneously trying to drum up financial support for my foreign ministry.

I watched as the other missionaries seemed to effortlessly raise the needed funds for where they were going, but I kept falling way short of that same kind of success. No matter how hard I tried or how much I traveled, I could not seem to interest anyone other than a few close friends in helping me. I tried hard for three straight years to make it happen, but the bottom line was, no money--no ministry. I even traveled back to Palestine the following year with my good friend and pastor, Carl Dixon, to have another look at the possible ministry opportunity. I put on a good front for my friend while we were there, but actually had other motives.

Although Carl and I had a really great time there in 1994, I truthfully began to see a disturbing trend that was not fitting very well with my dream. It seemed that I was not the first foreigner who had shown up to "save the Palestinians". I know that sounds funny, but the truth was that they had already had one too many bad experiences with egocentric "missionaries" blowing in and treating them like stupid children. No matter who I told my dream to, I kept getting the same look of distrust and discouragement. I was not at all receiving the hand of fellowship that I had envisioned. In fact, they kept telling me not to bother, and that they already had enough churches. I don't think that anyone was trying to be mean to me. I never met a single person over there that didn't like me. They were truly among the most hospitable people that I had ever met. But they had simply grown weary of the continual train of less-than authentic-brothers who kept arriving. Who could blame them?

Finally, in the summer of 1996, I traveled back to the Holy Land with a different kind of mission in mind. Having raised almost none of the financial support needed to sustain a full time missionary and with not one single person from Israel or Palestine willing to offer me a welcoming hand of fellowship for my proposed ministry, there was really only one thing left to find out. It had been three years since I had began pursuing this young lady's love and was at that moment no closer to a permanent relationship with her than the first day I had met her. The simple truth was that my heart could no longer take it. I needed to know once and for all if she loved me or if I needed to put this all behind me. She had never told me to get lost, so we just continued for those years to enjoy the same friendship that we started with. But she always kept me at arm's length when it came to her love. So I decided that it was time for her to surrender or tell me no. I bought a small ring and booked a flight. It was now or never. This all may sound very brave and romantic, but believe me when I say I was very afraid of the possible outcome. I arrived, returning to my familiar friends at the Bible College, where I always felt welcomed and at home. The next day I called her and we spent another two weeks visiting and catching up. Finally, toward the end of my visit, I collected the nerve to pop the question. I had just driven her back to her house after an evening out and was sitting there in the car saying goodnight. Then, to her shock and surprise, I just did it. I put the ring on her finger as I had seen done in every romantic movie that I had ever watched. I then told her that the pain in my heart had become too much for me to bear and that I was no longer interested in waiting for her decision. I asked her to marry me. She sat there stunned, just staring at the ring for what seemed like an eternity. Finally, she caught her breath and, to my dismay, she said no and gently slid the ring off of her finger. Handing it back to me, she cited the same familiar reasons that she had started with three years prior. She simply could not let go of her family and her home. We said goodbye and I drove away. I was crushed. I wept all the way back to the college and spent the rest of that night reflecting on those past three years.

"This too shall pass."

How could this have happened? Just then Heaven seemed to close its windows and doors to my anguish. No matter how much I cried out to God for an answer, I sensed no response. I continued to beg him for some help in understanding what now seemed to have been pure madness. But still I got no reply. Soon my desperation turned to anger. I quit asking for help in understanding and began demanding an explanation. As you can imagine, he wasn't at all intimidated by my blustery protest. Nor was he moved to action by my lame attempts at provocation as Job had done in antiquity. It seemed, at least for the moment, that he was quite willing to ignore my tantrums and allow my constant barrage of angry questions to rage on. I stayed angry at him for several months, despite the flood of consolation that my friends attempted to lavish on me. I simply refused to be consoled. My heart was broken and I was quite content sulking in my self pity and my anger. In my mind, I kept bringing the responsibility for all of this disappointment and pain right back to the feet of God himself. My indictment was short and sharp. He could have prevented this if he wanted to. He could have stopped me from running headlong into this mess three years ago if he really wanted to. How could he just let me go on and on believing in this fantasy? These accusations came with conviction, as if I was the first person to have ever accused God of being irresponsible and mean. I finally grew weary of yelling at him and provoking no response. So when spending the energy was no longer advantageous, I just slipped quietly into a total state of disappointment and depression. This was not good at all, because not only was God content to allow this agonizing drama to continue to teach me its difficult lesson, He now seemed eager to begin the next one as well. I had really never wrestled with true disappointment in God before and I found myself quite unprepared for how long this thing would drag on. My first breath of hope came only when my very wise and dear friend Tim Polak dared to approach me when others had gotten their heads bitten off for attempting the same. He knew me well enough to know that I was not just crying for attention and that I was in real pain. With the love and grace of the Lord Jesus himself, this friend came to me, placed his hand on my shoulder and said "I know that you are hurting Jim. Take courage, brother; this too shall pass." And although it certainly did not appear to be passing at that moment, he was right and I knew it. Thank God for such friends. I thank God that Tim didn't give up on me even though I was being a genuine pain in the neck to everyone during those months. Not long after that, God did begin to speak to his angry little man again. When the time was right--when he did finally begin to speak to me about all of this--he did so in a most undeniable way. It really did need to be as specific and over the top as it was so that I would truly have no doubt as to who was now doing the speaking. He literally used four men, who may have not even known each other, to say exactly the same thing to me in the span of just a few days.

In those days, I was in the habit of listening to Chuck Swindoll and Dr. James Dobson on my local Christian radio station each day. I still do as much as I can. This particular week, both of them were addressing the issue of disappointment with God. It seemed an incredible coincidence that two of the men whom I most respected and who quite literally had mentored me from a distance over the previous decade, were speaking directly to my pain. That evening, one of the young men from our Bible study gave me a book by Philip Yancey entitled Disappointment with God. I read it and discovered that Yancey was joining Swindoll and Dobson with the same message. Now, as if that grand trio wasn't enough to get my attention, God prepared the coup-de-gras. At that precise moment, one of our missionary families, Larry and Janet Gray returned from their latest four-year term in Africa for a furlough. This incredible family had just suffered unimaginable loss during those past four years on the Dark Continent, including the unexpected passing of their nine year old son while they were still out in the bush. As I sat listening to these giants of faith testify how God had just faithfully brought them through this season of tremendous loss and suffering, I wept with them and knew that I simply had to spend some time with them. That afternoon, I arranged to meet Larry at a friend's home. After some small talk, I revealed the purpose for my visit. Very carefully and without any lame comparisons, I told him how I had so deeply believed that God was taking me in a direction towards ministry in the Holy Land and towards true love. I then shared with him how it had all simply and without explanation evaporated before my eyes. I didn't have to talk long. He could see the pain eking through the lines of my young, sun-tanned face. He spent a few minutes praying for me and trying his best to encourage me. Then he said something incredible. He said "While our family was really suffering these past couple of years and when it truly seemed like God had simply abandoned us, we came across this wonderful little book that we could not get enough of. We read it as a family and then each of us took turns reading it for ourselves. It was just what we needed at that moment." I was now on the edge of my seat and at the end of my patience as I demanded "What was it?" His answer floored me. "It was a wonderful work by Philip Yancey entitled Disappointment with God." I was so profoundly moved by the events of that week at that moment, that I could no longer contain myself. I leapt straight up from the lawn chair that I had been sitting in and shouted, "NO way! I just read it! Wasn't it great?" We both laughed and discussed the book in detail for a bit. We ended our time together with more prayer and rejoicing, as we both contemplated the reality of two guys like us, wandering around in the plan of God. I was now thoroughly convinced that my heavenly Father had not abandoned me--and was in fact thinking about me and communicating with me right then.

The question had never really been where God had gone when life hurt. The more relevant question, as Mr. Yancey had so brilliantly pointed out in his book, was where had I gone? My generous heavenly Father had merely granted me a nice trip to experience the Holy Land, but before he could blink his eyes, I was gone. And no amount of calling me back or warning was going to reach me. I had suddenly and without ever consulting him for even a moment created this entire plan and put it into action. I alone was responsible for coming to the foot of that great and horrible mountain of disappointment. And I alone spent the next three years tirelessly climbing to its summit to taste its bitter reward. I was now returning with my scars and with my tail tucked between my legs, back to the very place where I had wandered off from the Shepherd of my soul. There I found him waiting patiently for me, eager to embrace me and heal my new wounds. With incredible graciousness, he never condemned me. He pitied me and then encouraged me with that great love of his. There was no need to chide me. My wounds--and the fact that I had returned to him with them--told the story of a young man who had truly learned his lesson. I have read Mr. Yancey's book a couple of times and I highly recommend it to you if you are hurting and are wondering where God is. I was now well on my way to recovering from that long season of deep disappointment.

CHAPTER TWELVE

HE GIVES GRACE TO THE HUMBLE

I SPENT MOST OF 1997 growing in my trade as a concrete finisher. This busyness, along with a couple of short whimsical dating excursions, helped to pass the time while my heart healed itself. I also started growing increasingly discontented with the regular income that I derived working for Verle. I wasn't trying to be ungrateful, but the truth is, there really wasn't much money in working for someone else. I also began to take notice of the money that Verle was making and the life style that it was affording him and started wondering if I should do the same. During that year, I decided to test my wings and take on a few small side jobs of my own. Verle, in his usual generous manner, assisted me with these jobs, taking no payment for his hard work. He did this for me a number of times during that year and began to sense that I wanted something more than just a job. I was too scared to just quit my job and start working for myself and besides I always believed "if it aint broke, don't fix it." None of this appeared to need any fixing and I was comfortably content to just leave things well enough alone. I figured that it was easy enough to just go on working for him and to happily take the odd side job as they came along. But Verle was too much of a friend to simply allow me to remain in that comfort zone. He knew that soon enough the time would come that he would have to push me out of the nest.

That day arrived in late September of 1997 while I was prepping one of my side jobs. As usual, he was allowing me to use his business supply accounts to order my materials and was helping me with the work. It looked like it was going to be a great month for me financially. Verle was busy and I had this side deal with several others waiting in the wings. Then he just said it. "You're working for yourself now. It's time to leave the nest so your new business can grow. I know you don't want to hear this, but Friday is your last day with me." It felt just awful hearing those words. The feeling was something of a mixture of being fired and being pushed off of the high dive at the swimming pool when I was a kid. But that was it. I was officially on my own. I immediately advertised my new venture in our local yellow pages and, to my great relief, the phone started ringing. Verle was right--my business wanted to grow, it just needed a chance. I don't get to see Verle as much as I used to. He is a good friend.

With the last vestiges of uncontrolled anger being snipped out of me and the cosmic disappointment issue finally resolving itself, a third and every bit significant deficit was about to be revealed in me. The thrill of being my own boss, coming and going at my leisure, was soon accompanied by a very different reality. It was not long before I discovered that the contracting trade in southwest Florida was an extremely fickle proposition at best. Some months flowed with brilliant prospects and plenty of income, while others were as dry as the Judean desert. This fickleness was as random as a roll of the dice and every bit as unpredictable. This created the perfect stage on which to expose my utter weakness in money management. I was great at selling the work when presented with a potential client. I also had no problem managing the job site and giving the customer what they expected. But mapping the company funds through the dead times was as foreign a concept to me as a walk on the moon. Luckily I was still single and without children at the time or they would have been forced to suffer this punishing reality right along with me. I would literally give no thought to money planning or budgeting. When the money was present, I paid my bills. Any extra was spent on world travel. When the money dried up for a bit, the bills simply had to wait. Not my suppliers and my helpers. They were always paid. It was my personal bills that suffered. This, of course, made me quite unpopular with the bill collectors during that period of my life. I can't number the times that my lights and phones were disconnected during that year. I even came extremely close to having my vehicle repossessed. It all finally came crashing down on me in early

1998. I was two months behind on my rent, along with everything else, when my landlord got creative. Knowing that I was a leader in my church, she called the pastor and told him about my delinquency, hoping that he would pressure me to pay up. He, in turn, told the elders. They all agreed that the issue needed to be addressed and that I needed to be called in. I guess they were as embarrassed as I was and offered to help me become a better manager of my finances. Since I was in fact a leader in the church, they had every right and responsibility to address the issue. I should have humbled myself and accepted their offer, but instead I became furious. I simply couldn't believe that my landlord had exposed my private trouble to the church like that. And that the pastor had told the elders infuriated me all the more. I was told in no uncertain terms that if I insisted on clinging to my pride and refusing their help, I would be asked to resign from leadership. They reminded me of what was clearly written in the word of God concerning the matter.1 Peter 5:5,reads "Likewise you younger submit to the elders, in fact all of you should be submissive to one another for God resists the proud, but gives grace to the humble." I needed God's help and their help as well at that moment and I knew it. I was just too angry and embarrassed to accept it, so I stormed out and refused to speak with any of them. I was then dismissed from every leadership position that I had held in the church--and rightly so. Don't mistake their actions with some kind of weird excommunication or invitation to leave the fellowship. These were simply the church leaders addressing another church leader. I got set down and I would have done nothing different had the roles been reversed.

Now that may sound trite or even insignificant to some. But to place it into a more relevant perspective, simply imagine being disqualified or removed from something that you dearly love and have worked diligently towards for years. That was it for me. There was nothing more important to me at that time than God's church and being a leader in it. As I sat there and reflected, I knew that all of that fierce devotion should have been focused on God himself rather than my position in the church or what others thought of me, but it wasn't. If it had been, I would have heard him when he reached out to help me. Instead I puffed out my chest and gave myself a front row seat to "God resisting the proud." It was really a sad sight to see. Financially drowning and humbled to the dust, yet still I persisted in my pride and anger. For months I just sat there in church burning in my anger, justifying my poor victimization and running ever farther from God's promised grace. My girl friend at the time decided that she wanted no part of this drama and broke up with me. Wonderful! But who could blame her? I literally felt like I was going to explode. Day after day I just sat at home staring at the walls and stewing in my anger. I was mad at the elders, I was mad at myself and, oh, yeah, I was once again mad at God. I know that he has seen no end to the line of angry children hurling accusations at him throughout the centuries, but it was once again my turn and I was just getting warmed up. One of my favorite verbal missiles was to compare God to my former stepfather. I honestly had no other point of reference when it came to envisioning true fatherhood. The only father figure that I had really ever known was a self centered, violent predator, who never cared at all for me. Consequently, during these periodic crises of faith it was never easy for me to see my heavenly Father in any other light than what I had already experienced. Of course, he was also an easy target. The terrible things that I said to God during those hard times were simply unconscionable. It was once again my good friend Tim Polak who came to the rescue. This guy could tirelessly listen to my endless angry rants about God's uneven handling of things and he could do so never uttering a word of disappointment or condemnation toward me. He could listen for hours before faithfully reminding me that God was not my stepfather. In fact he was nothing at all like my stepfather. With the passion of a true friend of God, he defended him and preached to me of his goodness and his kindness. Tim Polak never let me forget that God is no stepfather. The fact that I now rest in that knowledge is due entirely to that man's faithful friendship to me during the good times as well as the bad. Pray that God would grant you such a friend in this life.

Well, once again, this must have been God's target zone for my next crash landing, because crash I did. Why do we always need to end up in the prodigal's pig pen before we come to our senses? Remember the story of the prodigal son from the Bible?

It was about the arrogant boy, who after demanding his share of the inheritance from his father, left town and squandered the entire sum on riotous living. When the money was gone and he began to starve to death he was forced to take a culturally despised job as a pig tender. As he lay in the pig pen eating the pig's food to survive, he came to himself. He remembered his father and how even his servants had food to spare. He then humbled himself and journeyed home to ask his father to forgive him.

His father, who had been agonizing over the loss of his son, saw the ragged boy coming from far off and ran to him and fell on his neck. Before the son could even ask for forgiveness, his father forgave him and completely restored him to his place in the family. Sound familiar?

Could it be that God allows us to end up in a place as low as a pig pen, so that we would not be tempted to take the credit for our salvation from it? I think yes, but whatever the answer, there I was, neck deep in my own version of that pen. Every time I attempted to crawl out of it under my own steam, I just became more and more angry. One day, I got into my little pickup truck to run some errands. I was still fuming as I drove away from my home and still had several imaginary arguments simultaneously occurring in my head. I was winning them all too. Just then, as the boiling anger once again reached its zenith, I exploded. My entire face turned several shades of red as I let loose with yet another barrage of rage and profanities which caused me to nearly beat my steering wheel from its place. Just then, as it all once again reached critical mass, I heard a very familiar soft voice whisper to my soul "Don't go too far, son." Boom! Right in my face, just like that. Nothing more, nothing less, just "Don't go too far son." This was a fairly amazing--or should I say--startling phrase to hear at that particular moment because this was precisely what I was feeling at that particular moment. I literally felt as though I was about to cross some invisible point of no return. I knew he was right, so with a very deep sigh and some gritting of my teeth, I held out my hand as any drowning man would and prayed "Lord, please rescue me from me." I had not even finished that breath when all of that dark heaviness began lifting from me in its entirety. In an instant I was well. As well as Lazarus, whom Jesus had raised to life and who had just walked out of his tomb, after having been dead for four days. My face had not even finished recovering to its natural color yet, but I literally could not even remember what I had been so angry about. Once again, I had conclusively proven that I could not fix myself, but with one ounce of faith and humility, God ran to me and again rescued me. "And He gives grace to the humble." I can honestly say that I have lived that verse.

Immediately, I returned to my faithful church and began making my rounds asking for forgiveness and getting back to work. I also enrolled myself into a "Crown Ministries" finance class that our fellowship was sponsoring and, suddenly, I was on my way to sound financial stewardship.

Oh, it took some time to undo the years of poor habits and accumulated debt, but I had truly turned a corner at that point. Nearly fifteen years have past since that incident and each day I am still learning to be a better steward of what the Lord has given to me. But at least I now know who it all belongs to and I'm not going backwards any more.

CHAPTER THIRTEEN

LIGHTENING STRIKES TWICE

For the balance of that year, there seem to be no shortage of work, which meant that I was able to catch up on all of my bills. I was also able to pay my debts and even pay off my vehicle. Since there was such a surplus of income, I decided to take another journey to the Holy Land and this time I invited my old friend Jon Franson, who had invited me five years earlier. We agreed that we wanted to be in Bethlehem during Christmas that year, so we made it happen. December of 1998 was a marvelous time for Israel and Palestine. The first Intifada or Palestinian uprising against Israel had ended in 1993 and for the next five years something very akin to peace had begun to settle into that land. Palestine became abuzz with road construction and other infrastructure; to accommodate the growing throngs of tourists who were finding their way back after the fighting had ended. Bethlehem was preparing itself for the coming millennia celebration, Bethlehem 2000, and was quite the place to be if you were a Christian. We arrived a year too early for that particular celebration, but still I found the general atmosphere to be more jubilant than I had ever seen in any of my previous three visits.

The typical sandstone colored buildings which have lined those historic streets for hundreds of years had obviously readied themselves for the occasion. They were lovingly trimmed with all of the festive Christmas lighting and décor that one would find in any small town in America; but with one glaring distinction. In a trademark display of culture found only in that part of the world and on a hill out in the distance, you could also hear the song of a religious cleric, calling out from atop the local mosque as he summonsed the Muslims to prayer. And although they had nothing to do with Christmas, those frequent songs did have a way of adding to the authentic flavor of that magical place, at least for a visitor like me.

Now I had never been there during their cold season and things were quite different. During the summer months, the hard, dry wind which constantly whips up the dust from the Judean desert, gives the sky a hazy red tint. But December brings the rainy season and things change dramatically. The crusty dry earth begins to drink in the new moisture like some brittle old sponge. As all of that fresh, life-giving relief pours down, all of nature seems to rejoice as though it had been holding its breath anticipating its reprieve from the long dry summer. The once dusty streets take on a kind of postcard cleanliness, as they glisten with their constant coat of fresh rain water. Tons of airborne dust particles find that they can no longer resist gravity and are driven back to the earth from whence they came. The sky becomes as clear and blue in December, as it is in the tropics and the air is every bit as fresh. At night, the surrounding hills become ablaze with a thousand points of light, which mingle with the stars until the two become one. It is truly a magnificent place.

Jon and I rented a car at the airport in Tel Aviv and drove straight to the Bethlehem Bible College. It seemed that even they were expanding the borders of their tents. To my surprise, they had added a new multi-story guest house since my last visit. It was a marvelous addition, equipped with a new library and computer center to go along with their growing curriculum. Bishara and his staff were as friendly and hospitable as ever, graciously welcoming us once again. We were ushered to our room on the fourth floor, overlooking the town of our Lord's birth. The view from our room was breathtaking and offered a clear view across the valley to the hillside village of Beit-Jala. The breakfast room was on the other side of the building. From there, you could peer straight down Hebron road into the heart of Bethlehem. But from the rooftop you got the whole sha-bang; a windy panorama of it all. Many evenings you could find me just sitting up there, staring at the hills as if they were some irresistible piece of art.

Now I had neither seen nor heard from my aforementioned young lady friend for a couple of years. The extended time away from her, along with my agonizing lessons in finance and humility, had helped me put aside that painful episode. I was there to enjoy the Holy Land at Christmas with my friend Jon and that was it. At least I thought that would be it. This next bit will probably cause many of you to want to slap me across my head, but bear with me. It works out in the end. Shortly after our arrival at the college, I left our room and walked over to the main office to pay for our accommodations. I walked into the same office that I had walked into on so many occasions during previous visits, but something was very different this time. There, sitting behind her desk and waiting to take my money, was a new face--at least new to me. At that exact moment, there in that exact same town and in that exact same building, lightning struck me for the second time. Don't slap me yet. In my defense I am, after all just a guy, and as any guy can tell you, this brand of lightning always seem to target us at very peculiar moments indeed. Honestly, we can't help it. It just zaps us. Be that as it may, there she was, just sitting there and looking so very beautiful. She smiled and greeted me as if we were old friends and Zap! Once again, I was smitten. At first, I didn't recognize her, so I gave her my money, smiled back and got out of there. Good call, brother. OH my God, I thought to myself. What is the matter with me? I laughed and started back to my room. Just then, this beautiful vision chased me out into the hallway and "said "Excuse me, you're Jim, aren't you?" Now I was shaking in my boots. "Um yes, I replied. By the way, if you have to think for a second before answering a question as simple as "What is your name," you're either breaking the law or getting struck by that lightning. In my case, the answer was obvious. She kindly handed me some mail and said "These came for you recently." I thanked her again, at least I think I did, and then fled to my room. I was going to be there again for two weeks and, with my hyper romantic history, I had every confidence in my ability to get myself into another heart-wrenching situation in that short amount of time. Armed with this valuable wisdom, I decided to avoid her for the balance of the trip.

Jon and I left Bethlehem for a few days, driving north to Rama village near the Lebanon border. Our intentions were to visit our dear friend and brother, Makram Mesherky, who lived in Rama with his beautiful wife and two daughters; although they have since added twin boys to their family since this visit. Makram is both a student and a teacher of theology. He has also authored several books and has a brilliant mind for things eternal. I met him and his wife when Pastor Carl and I were there in 1994, while Makram was conducting a seminar near Bethlehem. I was truly looking forward to seeing them again, but planned to be back in Bethlehem in time for Christmas. We spent a pleasant two days enjoying their hospitality and doing some site seeing around the north end of the country before heading back for Christmas in the town of David. I had plenty of time during the long drive south to consider the young, beautiful girl I had seen a few days earlier. I decided that it wouldn't be so bad if I at least met her. You know, just to see who she was. Oh, really man, is that what we're thinking now? What happened to run for it? That was good stuff, brother and, if I remember correctly, it was working just fine for us yesterday. What happened? What changed? What in the world are you doing, man? If anyone out there can hear me, please slap him! (That's literally the way my conscience talks to me sometimes.) So I did what any young man would do in my position. I turned up the radio and ignored him.

Friends told me that her name was Olwen Awwad and that she was a very nice girl indeed. They gave me her phone number, telling met I should call her family if I wanted to meet her. I then went straight back to the college and called her.

Her family said that it would be okay if I came to meet them and gave me directions to their home. They live in the small town of Beit-Sahour, which is just a few minutes southwest of Bethlehem. In fact, it is the town where the famous shepherd fields are located. I was not at all familiar with that town and got lost a couple of times trying to find them. But with some persistence, I finally located Olwen's younger brother Nabil, who flagged me down and rescued me from my wandering.

The sitting room was full of people whom I had never seen before in my life. Olwen, her parents, aunts, uncles, family, friends and a dear missionary woman named Olwen Jones, who had literally been a part of their family for decades. She was actually the woman for whom Olwen was named. All of them were sitting there in a large circle laughing at the stunned look on my face. I had never done this "proper" family introduction thing before and apparently my nervousness was evident for all to see and enjoy. I managed to navigate the circle of handshakes without falling down or spilling anything before being shown to my seat. After a small barrage of friendly questions, Olwen invited me to a den next to the sitting room, where we could get acquainted. I had already decided to do things differently this time. I vowed to abstain from any talk of romance and would instead concentrate on simply meeting a new friend. It seemed that I had learned my lesson and was not so eager or hasty in casting my heart back into the sea of love. We talked for a long while before ended our time by exchanging phone numbers and email addresses. We then bid each other farewell. I was not about to put myself through another emotional train wreck, so I kept my head screwed on this time. No fantasies or sleepless nights, just a new friend; albeit an extremely beautiful new friend. Olwen was also a singer in the Bethlehem Bible College choir, so Jon and I ended our time in the Holy Land with a Christmas concert in manger square. Olwen's choir was only one of about seven or eight that performed that night. It was truly a grand evening and will probably be remembered as one of the best nights of my life.

"I will be waiting for you."

Well, Jon and I flew home and got back to our respective lives, which included our construction jobs and a great deal of fishing when we were not working. I actually worked very hard that year attempting to steady my fledgling new business, but the work was extremely fickle and often eluded me. No sooner would my business take flight and begin to soar when the winds of fortune would suddenly fail and I found myself grounded with no prospects. Not having been gifted with any real business sense, it was a reality that I was going to have to learn to live with if I intended to stay in this profession. Instead of taking classes and learning more about business management, I coped with the down time by fishing, dating and traveling more. I would simply lock the doors and enjoy my life until the next job availed itself to me. I know what you are thinking, but nearly a decade later, I'm still not really sure how I feel about all of that. With a little more wisdom I might have a thriving business by now, but I'm not all together sure that I ever really wanted that. Oh well, we live and we learn.

No matter what I found myself doing during the course of any given day, I would always end that day by checking my e-mail to see if Olwen had written. Such was our happy little friendship until the summer of 1999. Around August of that year, a small team of volunteers from Palestine journeyed to Oklahoma as part of the mammoth clean up and rebuild effort that was taking place there in the aftermath of the devastating F-5 tornado that ripped through that area the previous spring. Olwen was one of those selfless souls who came and worked day and night to help repair a family's damaged home. As soon as I found out that she was coming to the States, I began to plan a trip of my own to Oklahoma. I arrived several days after her and was invited to stay in the same home that their team was living in. I was able to spend a few short days with her and realized that our friendship had actually developed into something a bit deeper.

I knew that there would be no real face to face courtship since she was headed back to Palestine in a few days, so I decided that she was just going to have to get six months worth of dating, in one romantic evening. We took a walk that night and I apologized for having to do it this way. I then took a breath and cautiously laid my heart at her feet. I told her how I felt about her, which included the fact that I now wanted her to marry me. To my great delight (and relief) she picked up my heart and told me that she felt the same way. These were the very first romantic words that we had ever spoken to each other and the moment was very memorable. I then asked her to give me one month to tie up some loose ends and then I would come back to her country, speak with her father and officially ask her to marry me. Her words are still with me to this day. She said "I will be waiting for you."

I spent that month working every job that I could get my hands on in an effort to scrounge up enough money for the trip. I also needed to purchase an engagement ring, while still making sure that the bills were paid. With God's help, I did it and, in October of 1999, I found myself traveling back to the Holy Land for the fifth time. I proceeded to my home away from home at the Bethlehem Bible College, where I would spend my first couple of nights. My second day there, I went to Olwen's home and met with her parents, Nasr and Mary Awwad, two extremely bright and generous evangelical Christians. They welcomed me into their home with there usual dose of genuine hospitality and informed me that Olwen had not yet arrived home from work. So we enjoyed some tea while we waited. I then invited Nasr into his back yard where he patiently listened to my obviously prepared spiel before kindly granting me his blessing in asking for his daughter's hand. Everything appeared to be going as planned and all I needed now was for Olwen to actually say yes. She finally arrived and I asked her to go for a ride with me. I drove twenty minutes from her home in Beit Sahour to Jerusalem. We parked my rental, strolled leisurely through a busy open market district and made our way to the famous garden tomb. Once inside the garden, we found a quiet corner with an inviting little bench which was flanked by a couple of small shade trees and flowers galore. Her coy little smile told me that she too had been anticipating this moment. As we sat there face to face, I slipped that small ring on her finger and asked her to let me love her for the rest of her life.

She simply smiled and said that she would like that very much. And just like that, we were engaged.

Her friends were shocked and amazed at this surprise announcement and immediately threw us a traditional engagement party at the Bible College. With Arabic drums and women yelling and singing, the celebration went on for several hours before we thanked them and made our exit. After the party, Olwen and I spent the rest of the evening alone strolling down the famous Ben-Yahouda Street in Jerusalem as we discussed and planned our wedding. We both knew that we were going to be marrying into entirely different cultures, so we would have to plan delicately. I told her that we should have the wedding in her country and then throw a big reception upon our return to Florida. She and her family loved the idea and immediately set to work on the details. Everything seemed to be falling right into place until I was approached by an American friend who was working as a missionary volunteer at the college. He told me that although my wedding plans sounded wonderful, I might want to advise the American Consulate of our plans. I was obviously much more ignorant in these matters than I thought I was. I said to my wise friend "Why should I tell them anything? Once she marries me, she will be an American and we will simply go home together." My friend was most gracious in his response to my glaring ignorance and blind ambition and said "Yeah, but you might want to at least let them know so they can help you." He knew the hard news that I was in for, but didn't have the heart to tell me himself. I simply thought it was good advice and planned to obey his recommendation by visiting the consulate the following day. I arrived early and, after waiting in line for over an hour, learned that my meeting would be even shorter than I had anticipated. I briefly explained my wedding plans to the agent who was standing behind the bullet proof glass. His response was entirely less ambiguous than my friend's had been. He slid two pieces of paper under the glass and said "Congratulations. She will not be going home with you next week." He then explained the one detail that I had completely overlooked in this matter, which was immigration law. He told me that, wedding or no wedding, she was still going to need a visa to enter the United States. Our options were either a fiancée visa, by which she could come to the States and marry me there and then start the immigration process as a new spouse; or a new spouse visa, by which we could marry in Palestine as planned and she could, come to the States later after receiving the visa. Either way it would take six to eight months for her to receive a visa. Wow! This obviously put the brakes on everything. We sat down with her parents and discussed the options, finally deciding that the fiancée visa was the best way to go. We submitted the appropriate applications, devoted our love to one another and, with a long hug and kiss goodbye we started the waiting process.

I returned home and shocked everyone with the news. I had told no one of my plans for fear of having to again eat my words, so I felt that a surprise would be the best way to go this time. I spent the next year immersing myself in my business and transforming my home from a plain old bachelor's pad to a respectable home for my future bride. This was particularly useful in helping me pass the time and, before I knew it, I received word that she had been granted the visa and was preparing to travel. We chose November 18, 2000 as our big day. It was a difficult decision, due to the many exigent circumstances. For instance, we would have loved to spend time together planning the wedding details as a couple. That clearly wasn't going to happen. We also had to consider that we were expecting a number of her family members to be arriving with her. The fact that they would only be able to remain with us for a short time meant that the wedding would simply have to be very close to their arrival. This meant that I would have to do the lion's share of the planning and arranging without my fiancée even being in the country. I didn't mind it, but I soon discovered that I was not going to be able to accomplish this grand task on my own. Thankfully, just as I realized this and without any solicitation, dozens of my friends from our church came rushing in to rescue me. Or maybe they were rushing in to rescue Olwen, you know, by making sure that it all got done right. It was probably both. Anyway, they all pitched in and did all manner of wonderful things, which made our wedding a beautiful reality. I will never forget what they did for us.

Believe it or not, as if things weren't already challenging enough, the second Palestinian intifada came crashing onto the world's stage just a few months before our big day. The heated political situation between Israel and Palestine now meant that it would be much more difficult for Olwen and her parents to get out of the country, even though they had already been granted the proper visas. This new conflict came extremely close to spoiling our wedding day. The invitations had already been sent out and the church had been secured. There was no changing the date now. So we all just watched and prayed. To our great relief and joy, they made it out, though not before nearly costing Olwen's father his life. He literally defied an Israeli imposed curfew / closure, under threat of being shot on sight and made his way to the local government building to secure the proper airport pass. He was determined not to grant these two squabbling governments the opportunity of destroying his daughter's wedding, even if it cost him his life. I have seldom met two more thoughtful individuals than Nasr and Mary Awwad. They arrived at the Tampa International Airport late in the evening on November 1, just eighteen short days before the wedding. But she was here and that was all that really mattered. Her sister Vivian and Vivian's husband Majdy also arrived safely the following day and, to our joy and surprise, my old friend and Olwen's former employer, Dr. Bishara Awad also arrived and was eager to attend our wedding. That was a nice surprise.

Well the eighteenth arrived and the wedding was more beautiful than I had envisioned. Just like that, at the age of thirty four, I was a married man. One of the most amazing things about Olwen was that although she knew very well that she was not marrying into wealth and that she would have no one over here on this side of the ocean except for me, she still came. She was certainly better off financially right where she was. She was well-educated and already had a great career going. She lived at home with her parents and had plenty of expendable income, which she used to liberally bless others, while also finding time to travel the world with her friends. She was surrounded by dozens of caring friends and family and would have had no problem finding a good husband right there in her own town. Yet she chose me and I have never forgotten or taken that wonderful blessing for granted.

I knew that she was in for a rough first year, adjusting to a new culture as well as a totally different set of financial circumstances. I also knew that it was going to be my responsibility to be as loving and as kind as possible to her during this adjustment. It did not take very long for the honeymoon dust to settle and for me to realize that she did not share my same lighthearted enthusiasm about the frequent down time in our business. I tried to keep her jazzed about all the potential free time that we had while we waited on future prospects, but that down time genuinely troubled her and left her feeling, shall we say, less than secure. I tried to comfort her, but she was a woman and she had very different needs than I had. I had never been married before and was completely unprepared for what she was about to go through. It took some time for it to finally burrow through that thick male skull of mine, but I eventually got it. She needed her man to make her feel safe and secure and this little part-time construction gig just wasn't doing it for her. I told her that I finally got what she was feeling and assured her that I was willing to do what ever it took to make her feel more secure. I asked her if she would be willing to give the business just a little more time and that if it failed to grow to a place of constant support within a year, I would take a regular job. She wanted the business to grow as much as I did and hated the thought of seeing her new husband have to just lay it all down and go in a different direction, so she reluctantly agreed. Unfortunately, for most of 2001, things remained pretty much the same and she wasn't feeling any more secure. It was becoming painfully obvious that a significant career change was in my future. The reason I find it so necessary to use the word "painfully" in my previous sentence is due entirely to the fact that I am also forced to use that dreadful word "change" in my previous sentence. Honestly, does anyone like change, especially change that is forced upon them? Not me. I hated change of any kind which, as I now recall, has been the principle reason for most of my self-administered grief in this life. Oh, yeah, some guys just never learn. Anyway, the thought of a career change was a very threatening concept for me. It literally kept me awake most nights wondering just how someone my age might pull something that significant off. Then came the morning of September the 11th, 2001 and my wondering was instantly put to rest. It was a beautiful late summer morning. I was busy pouring a new concrete drive way for a customer and listening to some cool jams on my truck radio. Just before 9:00 AM, I was shaken to my core, along with the rest of the nation, by those awful terror plots that were beginning to unfold. I just stood there in total shock and listened for the next few minutes as nearly three thousand people were murdered in New York, Washington and Pennsylvania. As the first tower fell, I literally became sick. I could almost hear the collective screams of those who were falling into eternity. I spent the next few days weeping with the rest of the world and it seemed that my new career had suddenly been chosen for me. I discussed it with Olwen and we agreed that a career in law enforcement would be the appropriate choice. Two months later, we learned that Olwen was pregnant with our first child. So I spent most of 2002 pouring concrete and preparing for our baby's arrival. We were also busy plotting the course to my new career. In September of 2002 I was accepted and enrolled in the local police academy. About that same time, we welcomed our new baby boy into the world. He was a very handsome boy indeed, boasting his mother's good looks and his father's impatient disposition. As great as it was having him, it was no easy task having to pour concrete all day long and then get to the academy for the evening classes. The hardship was compounded by the fact that I had a wife and a new baby at home. But for the next nine months I never missed a class and was eager to hit the mean streets. I graduated as president of our class in June of 2003 and took the state certification exam the following month. After receiving the news that I had passed and was now certified by the State of Florida to be a law enforcement officer, I began applying at various agencies. On December 3, 2003, I accepted a position as a deputy sheriff with the Manatee County Sheriff's Office right here in sunny southwest Florida. I have been with the agency for several years now and have honestly never had a more satisfying job. Olwen also loves the job security and everything that comes with it, so we were both happy.

CHAPTER FOURTEEN

SO IT BEGINS

IT WAS DURING MY TIME at the Sheriff's Office that I received hundreds of hours of training on this subject and began to assimilate volumes of knowledge on behaviors and patterns of sexual predators and their victims. It was also during those years that I became painfully aware, in terms of shear numbers, of the actual scope of this world's assault on childhood. I don't mean the kind of watered down jazz that you can get from your local news reports either. I'm talking about the real sick stuff that you just never really hear about unless you have to deal with it everyday. But even more shocking than being bombarded with all of these dreadful images day in and day out was the bizarre reality that I myself was still trapped in that same old dingy cell of shame and denial that I had been languishing in forever. It sounds so crazy, but there I was in my forties, a big strong deputy sheriff attacking crime and yet still paralyzed and completely unable to divulge what had happened to me as a child. I really don't know how to explain it except to say that it had just become so darn easy to shut up and leave well enough alone. You know, just forget it and quit stirring up all those hornets of the past and all that. I had learned years ago how to forgive and move on. I reasoned that the past was the past and that was the end of all that drama. At least that's what I kept telling myself. It was only as a law enforcement officer that I discovered the disturbing truth that these predators never stop operating. For them, the past is the future also. I was astonished to learn that real predators can have numerous victims over a span of many years. This was a stunning revelation. It literally sickened me and provoked me to focus my energies in a new direction at work. In a twist of irony, I had become a law enforcement officer in the wake of 9/11. My new quest at that time was to do my part in protecting people from stupid murdering terrorist. Little did I know that I would actually be spending a good portion of my career protecting children from stupid raping terrorist.

During my first five years at the Sheriff's Office, I was assigned to the Patrol Division. While there I joined a squad of deputies whose job it was to assist our agency's Sexual Offenders Unit by monitor our local registered sex offenders. I still don't know whose brilliant idea it was to allow them to be set free from prison and live with us in our neighborhoods, but as part of their probation, they expected periodic unannounced visits from us. We would show up from time to time and check to make sure that they were behaving and not looking for another victim. We asked if we could check the interior of their homes, cars, sheds and garages for any signs that children had been there. We were also looking for any paraphernalia that they were prohibited from possessing. Since they were to have absolutely no contact with children we also visited their neighbors, particularly the ones with children, inquiring about the monster next door. If a child went missing in our community, these were the first homes we went to during our search. The rules that these people have to live under are strict and unambiguous. The slightest violation or sign of uncooperativeness with law enforcement and back inside they go (and you can bet that we were watching). I was also a field training officer back then and diligently taught this information to our new recruits.

Later, I joined the Investigative Bureau of our agency and became a "Crimes Against Children" detective. It then became my job to investigate all manner of crimes that were being perpetrated against children, particularly sex related crimes and crimes of abuse or neglect. Many of the cases that came to me were just awful to read and would bring the average person to tears if they dared peak into the pages of these files. There were seven detectives in our squad that worked nothing but child related crimes. We all endured an unending stream of sex crime cases that just kept coming. The things that are secretly happening behind closed doors in our communities are really quite unbelievable. You really have to see it, I think, to believe it. Anyway, I spent those years pouring myself into finding child abusers and predators, but never thought to go after the one who had ruined my own childhood.

Then it happened. One day, while I was minding my own business, my youngest brother Carson called to inform me that he and his long-time girlfriend were finally planning their wedding. He gave me their date and wanted to make sure that we would be available for it. "Of course we will be there," I assured him. "What do you think? I'll clear my calendar if I have to. Why wouldn't your oldest brother be at your wedding?" I ribbed him a little about being too young before congratulating him and saying goodbye. On its face, it was good news. Wow! My baby brother all grown up and getting married. Wasn't it just yesterday that mom brought him home from the hospital? Now he's asking me to come watch him get married. Have I really gotten that old? Man, how quickly this life slips by when we're not paying attention. Anyway, I should have been ecstatic about his good news and the coming nuptials, but almost immediately I began losing sleep over the announcement as well as my commitment to be there. I ignored it for a few weeks, but eventually I was no longer able to pretend that it wasn't there. What in the world was bugging me about this thing? I couldn't quite put my finger on it, but in truth I was really stressing about this wedding. Then it hit me. I got this flash photo in my head of his father there at the wedding, laughing and enjoying himself. His father, the man who had raped and molested us for all those years, coming to the same party. Great! I thought about it for a minute and realized that this was definitely the origin of my stress. It had been more years than I could remember since I had last seen this fellow and I was sure that I wanted to keep it that way. Every way I played the day out in my head, it kept ending in a confrontation. There was honestly no way that I could be in the same room with him while he pranced around making nice as though he had never done anything wrong. I knew his arrogance very well and knew that he would not hesitate to approach me in front of others and try to make a conversation. To which I would not have responded politely. He would certainly retort with some ridiculous face saving comment and it would just get ugly from there. The answer to the dilemma was a no-brainer. I was not interested in ruining their wedding day, so I concluded that I should simply not be there. This was not something that I could just tell Carson over the telephone, so I extended him the courtesy of driving halfway across the state to meet with him in person. I bought him breakfast and laid out my dilemma for him. To this day, he does not know the extent of what happened to his older siblings (primarily because he does not want to know) and, although saddened by the news that I was not going to be there for his wedding, he seemed to understand my problem.

I had a two hour drive ahead of me and plenty of time to consider what had just happened. I could not believe that this guy was still walking around breathing free air after everything he had done. And that I was now going to miss my brother's wedding because of him got me fuming. I stewed on that for a while, and then it just hit me. Why is this child rapist still free? He had probably perpetrated his crime against other victims over the years and was likely to continue in the coming years, yet still he was walking around breathing my free air. Why? Why? I'll tell you why. Because I hadn't prosecuted him yet, that's why. As quickly as that thought crossed my mind, I was instantaneously released from that old prison of shame and denial. Just like that. I stood up tall and kicked that old rusty cage door as hard as I could and discovered that it had been unlocked the entire time. I shook off those chains like a bear shaking off water and simply walked out. All those years of feeling guilty about bringing it up and, just like that, I no longer cared what anyone thought about it. It was time to make this fellow answer for his crimes, even if it hair-lipped the world. It was also time to permanently deny him the possibility of any future victims. Oh, yeah, it was most definitely time.

Suddenly, I was on fire with a mission and time was literally of the essence. I had to work quickly to eliminate even the possibility of another child falling victim to the same things I suffered. Instead of driving home, I drove straight to my Brother Eli's house. I told him what had just happened to me. The look on his face was pure relief and he immediately agreed that it was time to tell our story to the authorities. I then drove an hour south to mom and Sarah's home and had the same conversation with Sarah. She was also happy to hear the news and agreed that the time had surely come. Regardless of how many worlds were about to be shaken, it was clear that we held the moral high ground and no longer feared anyone's opposition. We all three sensed the imperative of the moment in bringing an end to this clown's reign of terror--so we got busy.

My position at the sheriff's office afforded me great connections in the agency's command staff and the State's Attorney Office. I had also worked directly under the sergeant who was currently supervising the agency's Crimes Against Children Unit, the unit that I would later come to work at as a detective. So I began setting up meetings, one after another.

First I went to the State's Attorney's Office and spoke to one of the felony prosecutors Mrs. Darlene Ragoonanan. I had attended the police academy with her husband, Renny and we were friends. After she had sat there in that meeting and listened to my horrifying story, she was able to advise me on appropriate actions. She put me in contact with their Crimes Against Children prosecutor. I then advised my immediate supervisor of what was coming and why. I did this primarily because I work for an elected official and wanted this information to filter through the chain of command and reach his ears quickly so that he would not hear it for the first time from some reporter, without any idea how to respond. I then went to our Crimes Against Children Unit and spoke to my former supervisor. All of these officials seemed to know how humiliating this was for me and extended more compassion than I had hoped for. We determined that there were four states and six jurisdictions that these crimes had occurred in, while discussing the best way of letting all of these other agencies know what they needed to know so that they could begin their own investigations. I took blank affidavits to Eli and Sarah and went home with one of my own. We all then quietly recalled and set to public record the atrocities that had occurred to us as children. We were writing things that we had given no thought to for decades and the memories that we were dredging up were dreadful, especially at night. After reliving all of that pain, we reassembled at the sergeant's office and were sworn to the testimony of our affidavits. I knew that our lives were possibly about to change with trial after trial now pending and with every embarrassing detail of our childhood about to become front page entertainment for more people than I dared to consider. As I handed over my affidavit to the sergeant, I looked at Eli and Sarah and said "So it begins."

CHAPTER FIFTEEN

THE REAPER

I HAVE PLAYED A FAIRLY important role in so many trials in my community that I cannot remember the number; some petty and others quite felonious. If there is one thing that I have learned in all of this, it's that the wheels of justice never turn as quickly and as neatly as we would like for them to. For instance, I have actually arrested people for armed robbery and waited more than a year before I saw the inside of a court room to begin proceedings on the matter. Now as frustrating as it sounds, that is the way our criminal justice system works in affording both sides the time that they each need to prepare their cases. The heavier charges obviously require more preparation time, so I knew that getting six agencies on the same page and ready for this trial could literally take years. Couple that with the fierce defense that the perpetrator would most assuredly mount and it could realistically be two to three years before this all came before its first judge and jury. This all began during the first week of April, 2007. After submitting our affidavits there was little for us to do except wait for the impending arrest and subsequent trials. Eli and Sarah would ask me from time to time what was happening with the case and I would simply remind them of the time that was needed to prepare. It was an unsettling anticipation for all of us, to say the least.

During this process several people began to inquire as to why it took so long for us to say anything about all of this. The simple answer to that question, which has now been thoroughly answered within the pages of this book, had been sealed away in my head for decades. But it was now becoming apparent that more that a few people were feeling a bit perplexed and would probably want an answer to that question, especially if I intended to silicate their assistance in the rescue of other victims. I was suddenly convinced that these mysteries needed to be completely revealed to the public by someone and I don't mean in half measures and watered down testimony. But who would do it? Who would tell it the way it really needed to be told? Who indeed?

In that initial meeting with my friend, Darlene at the State's Attorney Office, I recall the puzzled look on her face as I disclosed these horrible events. We had worked together on a few cases already and she held me in some esteem as a law enforcement officer and a prosecuting witness. So I could see why she was obviously finding it difficult to understand the timing. My response to her, although completely unrehearsed, would in fact be the mechanism that planted the seed for this book in my mind. I said "Councilor, for terrible reasons that I will write a book about later, we have felt compelled to remain silent until now." As we continued and eventually finished our conversation, I could not get that thought out of my mind. Where did such a thought come from? Write a book? I had never in my life entertained such a pious ambition as authoring a book. And although I had never excelled in academia as I should have, the inspiration, I assure you, was quite robust. From that moment on the birth of this project was imminent and, in April of 2007 I began to pen an orderly account of the ugly events of my childhood. Included for the record was my obvious survival of those events and the God-given fruitful and happy life which I have had the privilege to enjoy since then.

A vigorous new determination had seized upon me and was obliging me to this action. I felt determined, even driven to finally offer an unobstructed view behind the dark veil which had once kept these atrocities so well hidden. In doing so, I felt hopeful that others who were suffering the same nightmare might be more quickly rescued. I also wished to demonstrate to those who had escaped, as I had, the assurance that they too could live a life free from their past: one every bit as happy as the life that I was now enjoying. Finally, I hoped that these horrifying revelations would help bring catastrophic change to the way that some of our legislators and judges were viewing this epidemic with such indifference; and in their eventual handling or lack of handling of these predators. I was altogether unsure if any one would really be interested in hearing or reading such graphic information, but if there was even the slightest possibility that one fellow human could be helped, then the work and humiliation would be worth the effort. This would be my contribution to mankind and I would pray that it would find its way into the hands of the people who would be encouraged by this testimony--and into the hands of the people who were the most ready and able to start making these changes. May God grant it.

Seven months came and went like a watch in the night and suddenly, it was mid-October, 2007. I was still only halfway through this grand project of mine and felt no rush to finish, having never been an author before. I awoke on this particular day at my normal hour and greeted the day in the same manner that I had for the past forty-one years. All early indications suggested another normal day of fighting crime out on the mean streets of the west side. I shuffled to the kitchen for a glass of water and to check my phone messages. I was shocked to find numerous messages from my brother Eli. He had been calling me all morning, so I feared that something may be wrong. At that time, I normally finished my regular work shift at three o'clock in the morning and would usually sleep until around noon. I kept the phones far away from me so that the regular day time phone calls wouldn't wake me up. I called him back right then and could immediately hear in his voice that something very heavy had happened. His first chilling words caught me so by surprise that I was literally rendered speechless for half a minute. He said "Jimmy, Devlin was murdered last night. You need to call Carson." After taking a few moments to process what I had just heard, all I could get out was "What?" He repeated himself and I said "Are you sure? What happened? Where did this happen? Where is Carson?" "Slow down" he said. "Carson is with Glenda (Devlin's Girlfriend). I'm hearing that Devlin was at some poker game over in Vero Beach last night. The game was supposedly interrupted by an armed robbery. During the robbery, Devlin was shot and killed" Then he ended with "Jimmy, Carson needs us." I told him to get ready and I would pick him up in a couple of hours. I then hung up and just stared out the window for a few minutes, partly wondering if I was in the middle of some bizarre dream or if I had actually heard what I had just heard. I took a deep breath and began to think like a cop. I picked the phone back up and called the Vero Beach Police Department to speak to the detective who was working the case. I explained to her that we were preparing a sizable case against Devlin and gave her some of the details. I told her that I was concerned that he had many years to prepare for what he must have known was eventually coming. If he had somehow found out that I had actually begun his prosecution, I would not have put it past him to stage such an elaborate hoax and take flight. I requested that before anything was done with the body, an absolute and positive identification be made to determine that Devlin was in fact the victim. She understood and assured me that it would be done. I packed a few things, drove to Tampa to get Eli and we took off to Daytona.

It was another long drive with plenty of time to consider the ramifications of this strange turn in circumstances. I had just spent months preparing myself for a considerable amount of public humiliation which would be accompanying the coming trials. And just like that, the trials were gone. The waves of relief that were washing over me were genuinely magnificent. Not only had the coming humiliation just been erased, but the certain life interrupting multi-state trials had just evaporated also. As bad as this may sound, I could not help but also realize that Devlin had just received more justice than I ever considered he would.

We reached our destination and spent the next couple of days doing our best to comfort our baby brother. I must admit that it was a strange contradiction with which my brain had to cope, as I witnessed people actually mourning this man's death. I struggled to contain myself as this unjustified tearful dance played itself out before me. A part of me wanted to stand up on a chair and yell out "He was an unrepentant, egotistical, self-centered child rapist who never did anything good for anyone but himself! What in the hell are you people crying about?" But they didn't know what had happened, so I kept it together. While juggling that frustration with the very real need to comfort my brother, I was suddenly struck with more eternal realities which began flashing across my mind from out of the past. I recalled how I had read that forgiveness was one of God's principle instructions to his new church. I then remembered how he had instructed me nearly fifteen years prior to forgive my enemy, Devlin. Of course my first attempt was the old "I'll forgive, but I'll never forget" routine. That held me for a little while, but eventually I had to face the reality that God was actually calling me to something infinitely higher. He was calling me to true forgiveness. But *forgiveness* has never been an easy thing for us; has it? In fact forgiveness has always been a kind of stumbling block in society. We seem to always equated forgiveness with some strange demand from on high that the evil-doer should be allowed to get away with his crime, while the rest of us just go along as though he had done nothing. Although it does not mean that at all, I will admit that it surely does feel that way sometimes. In fact, forgiveness on any level may be the hardest thing that I have ever seen humans struggle to submit to. It literally took years for me to understand what God was wanting from me in regards to forgiveness and what he was promising in return.

The quote from the Old Testament book of Deuteronomy that "Vengeance belongs to God" was also repeated in the New Testament letter to the church in Rome, Romans 12:9-19.

"Love must be sincere. Hate what is evil; cling to what is good. Be devoted to one another in brotherly love. Honor one another above yourselves. Never be lacking in zeal, but keep your spiritual fervor, serving the Lord. Be joyful in hope, patient in affliction and faithful in prayer. Share with God's people who are in need. Practice hospitality.

Bless those who persecute you; bless and do not curse. Rejoice with those who rejoice; mourn with those who mourn. Live in harmony with one another. Do not be proud, but be willing to associate with people in low position. Do not be conceited.

Do not repay anyone evil for evil. Be careful to do what is right in the eyes of everybody. If it is possible, as far as it depends on you, live at peace with everyone. Do not take revenge my friends, but leave room for God's wrath, for it is written: "It is mine to avenge; I will repay, says the Lord."

It's really the same in any language. We simply can't have everyone running around acting as the judge and dishing out vengeance as they see fit. That is why every society sets restraints on its people and tries to exercise some form of due process over its law breakers. Now where do you suppose that idea came from? The answer is God, of course. The only difference lies in the motive. We restrain for the preservation of our civilization. God, on the other hand, although preserving civilization, restrains for the freedom of the individual. We have seen throughout the ages how the soul who refuses to forgive binds only itself with cancerous chains which eat away at its life day by day. This unforgiveness does nothing to punish the perpetrator and only allows his crime to continue its painful attack on the victim. This extended torment has even at times changed the very personality of the victim. The once kind and understanding soul can grow bitter and unhappy. Once bitterness has had its way with them for awhile, they find themselves doing things that they never dreamed that they were capable of doing. Some even end up committing the same violent acts on others that had been forced on them.

God knows this. He is like a loving father who knows important things about his children which they themselves are still too young to know. His command to forgive was never meant to excuse the criminal. No, his future is in the hands of the one who judges all things correctly and from whom nothing is hidden. His command to forgive was rather for the benefit of his injured child, that they would not find themselves enslaved to a never ending cycle of bitterness and revenge.

Forgiveness was the foremost ingredient in my own healing. Without it, no other attempt at becoming whole would have succeeded in overcoming the darkness. Forgiveness sets the wounded party free. I had given up my right to take revenge on the criminal who had harmed me and I have never regretted that decision. Now, I'm no fool. I know very well that this fellow's crimes were not some small one time misdemeanors. He was a real live child predator and these guys never stop looking for their next opportunity. What needs to be done with them in the criminal justice system has nothing to do with personal forgiveness and everything to do with society's stewardship and protection of its citizens--especially the very young ones. These criminals have proven that they are neither willing nor capable of governing their own lives, so society must step in and govern their lives for them. And since they are opportunistic predators, they simply must be warehoused away from any and all opportunities.

I wasn't prosecuting Devlin out of any lust for revenge. I had simply been awakened to the horrifying reality that there would very likely be additional victims if I did not. After that realization, it was only a question of how quickly I could get him off the streets. Devlin was a coy little man, who often boasted about his secular humanism. And in his boasting, he had often criticized mom for her persistent church going. In a side note, that is why it was so utterly ridiculous to see him standing in that hospital hallway crying out to God with deals and bargains while Rebecca lay dying in the next room. Of course, we were all praying for her, but his self-centered cries never made it through the ceiling tiles. He had convinced himself that he could do as he pleased in this life and that, as he neared the end, he would have sufficient time to again cry out with deals and bargains and perhaps save himself from damnation. I'm sure that he never imagined in his worst nightmares that he would die instantly during a violet crime and have no time to change his mind. Psalms 1:4 states it best. "*The wicked are like chaff that the wind blows away.*" I have always taken that to mean that they are not safe and that any moment may very well be their last. That robbery at that poker game was Devlin's last moment. He had chosen his path and I have chosen mine--and mine was the path of forgiveness.

CHAPTER SIXTEEN

LESSONS LEARNED

PLEASE LET ME EXTEND TO you my sincere gratitude in allowing me the privilege of briefly coming into your life with this excruciating story. You doubtless discovered within the first few pages of this book that I am no extraordinary fellow. But having been forced to cope with such extraordinary crimes, I felt it imperative to share what I had learned from a life lived in the fire. Indeed, I feel it incumbent upon me even now to leave you with relevant and useful information, lest this little project of mine simply vanish from the earth as yet another exercise in futility. What have I learned from this travesty? What can I give to you in view of the horrors that we have just witnessed throughout the pages of this book?

Item number one

I cannot emphasize enough the important role that a loving and caring family plays in the lives of very young children; both immediate and extended. The love shared and the values taught have a strange way of becoming their very backbone as they grow and mature. In fact, these virtues became the very cornerstone upon which my survival was built after being separated from my family. Those afternoons on the living room couch with Grandma Kincer and her Bible have literally stretched decades into the future and have guided me to the very place that I am today. They have both given me the courage and the vision to continually take the high road despite what had befallen me. I am living proof that a person can pass through such a hellish crucible and still be a happy, healthy, well balanced, honorable, contributing member of society. The desire to become more than what I had witnessed in Devlin was, in fact, being drawn from the rich memories that I had gained long before ever meeting him. Now if these virtues had such positive and profoundly enduring effects on me, I could only imagine the benefit that they would provide to a person who had been blessed with a life less tragic.

It is also noteworthy that these family members were the first to notice or suspect that something terrible was occurring to us. With statistics suggesting such an alarming number of violent sexual crimes being perpetrated against children today, family members have the potential of being their best, first line of defense. Don't be afraid to take the needed time to be observant, especially if you suspect that a child is being victimized. Don't be afraid to build a healthy relationship with that child, either. Please don't cover your eyes and hope that someone else will do it. You very well may be their only hope. This will foster a couple of important necessities in his or her life. First of all, this "healthy relationship" will model normal and healthy behavior for the child, giving them an important frame of reference from which to judge good and evil. They will very much need this in order to become convinced that what is happening to them is very evil and not at all normal. Secondly, it allows the child to garner a safe place to open up and ask for help. Keep in mind that a true predator will recognize your attempt at such a relationship and may do their best to isolate the child from you. Do not allow it. Please be persistent. The suspect only tips his hand with such covert behavior. Finally, never be afraid to get the authorities involved if you truly suspect that a child is being abused. Law enforcement and child protection agencies have become exponentially better at listening to the voices of reason in their investigation of such allegations. Most of the changes that I will be suggesting have to do with fostering a stronger and safer mind set within the child victim, so that at every turn in their life they will begin to see that they are not standing alone in this crisis. That it is rather the perpetrator who is the one standing alone against the world, rendering his venomous threats far less potent. Family is the place where these ideals and virtues will first begin to take root.

Item number two

As much as I hate it, many marriages are still ending in divorce these days. We all know that it will be the children who suffer the most during these breakups, both in the short term and over the long haul. Before the ink has dried on the divorce papers, the children become at risk. At risk of what you may ask. Well, at risk of mom or dad's next relationship, of course. Now I know that many couples have found safe, healthy and meaningful relationships after a divorce, but I'm not discussing these. I fear the ones who rush headlong and uninformed into their next affair, inviting unspeakable danger into their own lives and into the lives of their children. Please, do yourself a favor and take whatever time is necessary to really know the person that you are inviting into your lives; if not for yourself, then at least for the little ones. My wife and I knew each other only as friends for nearly a year before we ever discussed marriage. Do a little research and find out who this person is. If you don't, you may well regret it. I can guarantee you that my mom wishes that she would have taken this advice in 1970.

I suggest that you get to know their family and friends and begin digging around in their past a bit. Is their past really any of my business you may ask. You better believe it is, especially if you are planning to share your future with them. Most healthy, normal prospects will abide such probing in an attempt to signal that they have nothing to hide from you. They absolutely should be showing an active interest in building a new bond of trust. I couldn't wait to expose my future wife to all of the people in my life. I knew that they would not hold back and, in doing so, would make her feel more comfortable about the man that she was falling in love with. Beware of the prospect who attempts to conceal their past or isolate their friends and family from you. This, of course, does not automatically expose them as a child predator, but it should be throwing up enough red flags for you to, at a minimum, question the true character of this individual; in other words, justifying a closer look at this person before committing your life to them. Just remember that no prospect is ever worth forfeiting your own safety and the safety of your children. It's hard to get your kids back once you've thrown them to the wolves. Even if you do get them back, they will not be the same children that they were the day before. Please be careful.

Item number three

Discovering and exposing a child predator can be a very difficult thing to accomplish. Even though we will occasionally find one who possesses a lesser intellect and who literally gets caught in the act, these are few and far between. Most know very well how to stay off the radar and conceal their criminal behavior. Predators come in every size, sex and skin color. They adhere to no particular geography or economy and can literally be found in every corner of society. Dismissing the possibility that you have discovered a predator based solely on any of these factors is unwise. The fellow who devoured our childhood was a well dressed, college educated, small business owner. When our mother met him, she thought that she had found a winner. But he was no different than any other predator in the world. To succeed in their endeavors, they must become masters of stealth and camouflage. So it is going to take a concerted effort and a little thinking outside the box for us to trap them and bring an end to their malfeasance.

Let's consider for a moment a fellow who has gone on safari deep into the great African wilderness, with his mind set on hunting and slaying a lion. Once there this man would do well to resist any temptation or waste any time straining at the bush in his attempt to catch a glimpse of the great beasts. They are far too stealthy and well hidden. They will likely catch a glimpse of our hunter long before he knows that they were even in the area. Instead, it may be a better idea if he were to first locate the lion's prey and watch them. Their behavioral *changes* would teach him volumes about the presence of the predator. I believe that the same can hold true in the human realm. Most predators are acutely in tune with their environment and seldom let their guard down. They just seem to know when someone is sneaking up on them. Instead, pay attention to the behavioral patterns of the children in the area. At age four, I went from being a noisy, outspoken, extravert of a child to a frightened, introvert almost over night. It was a remarkably noticeable change in me which should have at least raised some concern in the adults around me.

Now let's look back at our lion hunter for a moment. We see that he has now changed his strategy and has located a nearby heard of impala. With a little stealth of his own, he has hunkered down to watch them. He watches as they graze and drink in peace, while their young leap and play with all of their heart under these quiet circumstances. He notices no signs of nervousness when a heard of zebra enter the same field and begin to graze nearby. Nor do the impalas display any edginess when some giraffe, buffalo and wildebeest come bustling onto the scene. But let the lion get within a hundred yards of them and things change dramatically. Any doubts that you may have been entertaining about who the predator was out there, would instantly be put to rest. In much the same way, if there is a predator stalking and preying on children in your family, then the children's behavior may be the key to alerting you to their presence. You may observe a strange avoidance of a certain individual or perhaps an inordinate fear of that person. Ask yourself why. Why is this outgoing child who is afraid of no one, suddenly avoiding or afraid of that one person? Why does their behavior abruptly change when that person makes the scene? Why is there such a weird dynamic between that child and that adult?

If something seems to be out of the ordinary, weird, or strange, then please by all means, **look into it**; covertly at first, if circumstances allow for it, but head-on if necessary. Who cares what the person in question thinks about it; you're not going to kill anyone by checking things out a bit. Check on the kid! For God's sake, forgiveness is easier than permission. You can always say "sorry" if necessary, but don't fail to look into that weirdness. Your instincts often serve you well and you know it. Don't doubt them now.

Ironically, I may not even be speaking to the other parent in this situation at all. I may of necessity be speaking to some other relative or individual from outside the family. I can't remember the number of mothers I have met who, for whatever reason, have either known that their children were being abused and did nothing to save them or who, upon finding out, began covering for the perpetrator. Who knows? Maybe they are genuinely afraid themselves or maybe they're just afraid that their lifestyle is about to take a detrimental turn. Either way, help for the victim will often have to come from outside their immediate family.

Keep those tender lines of communication wide open with the children whom God had planted in your life and keep listening to them. Not listening to them can have devastating consequences. Kids won't always tell you that someone is hurting them in the way or in the timing that you believe that they should. This is a very messy business and child victims seldom know who, if anyone can be trusted with their secret. I could have told you this decades ago, and investigators and prosecutors are finally getting it as well, that children are often genuinely afraid to tell on their tormentors. There is no cookie cutter way in which children will disclose their need for help. We may ask a child if they are being victimized and have them flatly tell us no, even though they are being molested regularly. This poor kid still trusts the perpetrators threats more than the police who are sitting right there wanting to help them. Some children will tell us that someone is hurting them and then take it back. These kids feel that they have just stirred the hornet's nest and believe that it is their responsibility to calm it all back down before the perpetrator makes good on his threats. Other children may begin disclosing in increments. In other words, even though they have been raped repeatedly for years by a perpetrator, they will test the waters by saying something minor like "He's messing with me." You may think, now what does that mean? Why don't they just tell me plainly what they mean? Believe me, they're trying. He's messing with me is simply their watered down version which they masterfully use to gage your reaction. As I mentioned earlier, they are desperately seeking out a safe ear to whisper into.

In addition to keeping an eye on their behavior, keep a vigilant watch over their body as well. If you are alerted to any new or strange pains in their private areas, then please have a look and let a doctor have a look as soon as possible. I don't mean the doctor in the emergency room either. No offence to them, but they are usually not equipped to look for signs of "past" sexual activity. Law enforcement usually gets a forensic specialist involved. Your child may be too afraid to tell you that someone is hurting them, but their behavior and their body will often speak for them. We just need to be paying attention. I doubt very much that the lions would stick around and continue to hunt in the area if they figured out that they themselves were being hunted.

Item number four

Breaking the gag of silence in children who are being abused is going to take a concerted and multi-faceted approach on all our parts. Getting child victims to "tell on" their abuser has always been the best way of exposing and prosecuting abuse. But children have always been handicapped by that great barrier of fear. The abuser, who is in truth weak and cowardly, seems so menacing and capable to their child victim. Of course, using this to their advantage, they are usually quite efficient in keeping the victim quiet for extended periods of time. I fear that this may continue to be a veritable fortress of protection for abusers everywhere; unless we begin to introduce significant encouragement to these children from outside their circumstances. I've already touched on the importance of family members creating an environment where children can begin to feel safe and confident in the face of an abuser's threats at home. But now I would like to suggest elevating that concept to an extreme level.

Prior to the devastating murders at Columbine High School, the atmosphere regarding the security of our children wasn't nearly as robust as it is today. The fundamental way that we look at school security, took a nationwide quantum leap forward after that dreadful event; and rightly so. It's a shame that it usually takes a terrible event to get us moving in a smarter direction, but that tends to be our nature. I am of the opinion that there have been more than enough children raped, abused and killed to now warrant that same sort of comprehensive change in the way we address this problem.

Get caught with a weapon on any school ground in America today and you will be arrested, charged with a felony and expelled. It doesn't even have to be a gun. Parents and school boards all across the United States have taken a firm stance with a "zero tolerance" for even the remote possibility of that sort of school violence. Metal detectors and a constant police presence on campus is now the norm in many schools. But quite possibly the most significant change that I have seen in this new "war on school terror" is the way that schools are now aggressively gathering intelligence. They are accomplishing this by winning back, as it were, the hearts and minds of the students. We have seen, in addition to the sweeping reform in school security, a noticeable relaxing in the student's long held, tight lipped no snitch policy in regards to this subject as well. Whereas a kid may never tell you who it was that vandalized the school, they will not hesitate to inform on a kid who even talks about bringing a weapon to school. It's no mystery as to why. They don't wish to be the next one caught by surprise during fifth period math class by some lunatic appearing in their doorway, spraying bullets all over the room.

Do you remember what it was like to travel by airplane prior to September 11th, 2001? I do. Non flying family members could accompany you to the very door of the ramp if they wanted to and the security check wasn't much more than a walk through a medal detector and a ride through the x-ray machine for your carry on. No one ever asked for my shoes or confiscated my bottle of water. Now, let some one stand up on a plane and aggressively walk toward the cockpit and see if fifty men don't stand up with him and adjust his attitude. Why? Because they don't wish to be on the next plane that some hijacker intends to crash into a building. So we as a society have taken very serious measures and think very differently now about flight safety than we used to. I believe that the time has come for us to make the same sort of changes in regards to preventing and prosecuting child predators. Some may baulk and cry that this is much ado about nothing and wonder why we are making such a big deal of this. But with numbers of victims as high as they are, believe me, it's already a big deal and time is literally of the essence.

I propose a more aggressive campaign of education all around. Children should be publically and regularly hearing about predators from the time they enter pre-school. Posters in the hallways, training, books, pamphlets, pictures and a regular barrage of healthy discussion should be the new norm. Kids should be learning all about the predator and his tricks from the earliest possible age. They need to be convinced as early as possible that no matter what the predator tells them, it's always okay to tell if someone is hurting them.

Finally, a word to my fellow investigators. I certainly mean you no disrespect. I know what it feels like to do your job. I know very well what it feels like to be lied to all day long and how difficult that can sometimes make it to believe the person who is actually telling the truth. It doesn't take long for this job to make us all a bit hyper-sensitive and cynical and that can be a good thing when it comes to our going home at night. But please never allow it to cause you to overlook a true victim who is standing in front of you begging for help. We are all they have.

As for me, well, it's now March 2012. Five years have passed since I started this little book and I am still very happily married to the same beautiful woman. Our previously mentioned rambunctious four-year-old son is now a healthy, rambunctious nine-year-old son. He is all boy like his father and he is making me feel my age. We still live in sunny Florida, where we hope to live out the rest of our lives. I am still very much free from those dreaded chains of shame and denial and life has never been better. I am still an active member of my church and loving it. I am also still a detective with the same agency investigating crimes committed against children. But more importantly than all of that, I am still daily responding to God's great love through his dear son, The Lord Jesus Christ and continuing to run with him into this great journey of life. I hope that what I have written has been a blessing and a help to you. The greatest thing that I can leave you with is this; never stop responding to God's love and he will never stop bringing you ever deeper into his great peace and healing. He loves you dearly and that's all that really matters.